EVERYONE
PLAYS
AT THE
LIBRARY

Creating Great Gaming Experiences for All Ages

SCOTT NICHOLSON

Medford, New Jersey

First Printing, 2010

Everyone Plays at the Library:
Creating Great Gaming Experiences for All Ages

 Published by Information Today, Inc., 143 Old Marlton Pike, Medford, New Jersey 08055.

Library of Congress Cataloging-in-Publication Data

Nicholson, Scott.
Everyone plays at the library : creating great gaming experiences for all ages / Scott Nicholson.
p. cm.
Includes index.
ISBN 978-1-57387-398-7
1. Libraries--Activity programs. 2. Games. 3. Libraries--Special collections--Games. I. Title.
Z716.33.N53 2010
025.5--dc22

2010010605

Printed and bound in the United States of America

President and CEO: Thomas H. Hogan, Sr.
Editor-in-Chief and Publisher: John B. Bryans
Managing Editor: Amy M. Reeve
Project Editor: Rachel Singer Gordon
VP Graphics and Production: M. Heide Dengler
Book Designer: Kara Mia Jalkowski
Cover Designer: Lisa Conroy

www.infotoday.com

Contents

Acknowledgments ... ix

Introduction ... xi

PART 1: Introduction to Gaming in the Library ... 1

Chapter One: Games and the Library's Mission ... 3

"What Do Games Have to Do With Books?" ... 5

Chapter Two: Games Versus Gaming Experiences ... 13

The Game Market ... 13
Focusing on One Game ... 14
The Game Versus the Gaming Experience ... 16
Questions to Consider for the Gaming Experience ... 18
Games in Collections Versus Gaming in Programs ... 19

Chapter Three: A Conceptual Model of the Library Gaming Experience ... 23

Model of the Library Gaming Experience ... 24
Gaming Experience Archetypes ... 27

PART 2: The Five Gaming Experience Archetypes ... 31

Chapter Four: Knowledge Gaming Experiences ... 35

Environment ... 36
Educational Games ... 37
Game Show, Trivia, and Party Games ... 38
Word Games ... 43
Big Games ... 45
Demographics ... 48
Library Goals ... 49

Chapter Five: Strategy Gaming Experiences 51
Environment 52
Abstract Strategy Games 53
Mechanics-Based Board Games 55
War Games 61
Card Games 67
Collectible Card Games 70
Digital Games 71
Demographics 76
Library Goals 79

Chapter Six: Action Gaming Experiences 81
Environment 81
Digital Games 83
Analog Dexterity Games 98
Big Games 102
Demographics 103
Library Goals 105

Chapter Seven: Narrative Gaming Experiences 107
Environment 107
Analog Role-Playing Games 108
Digital Role-Playing Games 114
Narrative Strategy Board Games 118
Big Games 124
Demographics 129
Library Goals 130

Chapter Eight: Social Gaming Experiences 133
Environment 134
Party Games 135
Strategy Games 137
Digital Games 139
Casino Games 142
Big Games 143

Demographics ... 144
Library Goals ... 146

PART 3: Putting It All Together ... 147

Chapter Nine: Planning the Gaming Experience ... 149
Determining Goals ... 149
Determining the Audience ... 154
Matching Goals and Audience to Archetypes ... 154
Selecting Specific Games ... 156
Creating Games ... 163

Chapter Ten: Facilitating the Gaming Experience ... 167
Preparing the Games ... 167
Preparing the Space ... 168
Preparing the Volunteers and Staff ... 169
Facilitating the Experience ... 171
Limiting the Choices ... 172
Putting It All Together ... 173

Chapter Eleven: Marketing and Partnerships ... 175
Reaching Out to Existing Patrons ... 176
Understanding Gamers ... 177
Marketing to Gamers ... 181
Holding a Regular Gaming Activity ... 182
Developing a Structure ... 183
Bringing in the Press ... 183
Partnering With Local Game Shops ... 184
Partnering With Clubs ... 185
Engaging Volunteers ... 186

Chapter Twelve: Assessment and Justification ... 189
Determining What to Measure ... 189
Using Measurements to Evaluate ... 198
Justifying Gaming ... 199

Chapter Thirteen: Keeping Up and Focusing on the Fun ... 201
Staying on Top of Gaming ... 202
Finding Reviews ... 205
Keeping the Programs Running ... 206
Considering Legal Issues ... 207
Conclusion ... 209

About the Author ... 213

Index ... 215

Acknowledgments

I would like to thank Ken Lavender for his ongoing support of my writing, which helps make up for my undergraduate degree in mathematics. I would also like to thank Jenny Levine for laying the groundwork for talking about gaming at a national level. Thanks also go to Jim Scheiderich and Bill Walton for reviewing the sections on war games and role-playing games.

I'd also like to offer thanks to the viewers and supporters of Board Games With Scott (www.boardgameswithscott.com). I've greatly expanded my perceptions on gaming through the connections I've made there. I offer a special thanks to Funagain Games for its ongoing support of Board Games With Scott and of games in libraries. In addition, I want to thank those of you in Syracuse who have put up with far too many of my wacky games.

I'd like to offer a big thanks to the expert panel that I've worked with through the Verizon Thinkfinity grant: Kelly Czarnecki, Liz Danforth, Christopher Harris, Lisa Janicke Hinchliffe, Terri Kirk, Allan Kleiman, Jack Martin, Dwight McInvaill, Eli Neiburger, Jennifer Nelson, Julie Scordato, and Paul Waelchli. These people, along with the leadership of Dale Lipschultz and the work of Jenny Levine and Beth Gallaway, have helped to provide many different perspectives on gaming in libraries that makes the construction of conceptual models possible. I would also like to thank Rachel Singer Gordon for her editorial work on this book.

Finally, I want to thank someone who I've gamed with for 20 years: Donald Dennis. He led me through many of my early experiences with gaming and has continued to be there as we've explored many different worlds together. But no matter how many times we've saved the universe, there's still someone in trouble.

Introduction

Games have always been an important part of my life. As a child, I spent many hours staring at a Chess board, engaging with others over board games, and controlling pixels driven by the Atari 2600 and TRS-80 Color Computer. In high school, I continued with these games and also got engaged in role-playing games, and during my free time in college, I got heavily involved in live-scale role-playing along with other forms of gaming. As I moved into my career, my time for gaming decreased, so I focused more on board and electronic games that took less time in one sitting.

I firmly believe that much of my success in life can be attributed to my gaming hobby. Different games test different skills—some mental, some physical, and some social. These games are similar to exercising in the gym: While you may not have the need to do an upright row in real life, the exercise helps strengthen parts of the body that may not get a regular workout so that your body can respond to real-life situations. Games work the same way: While you may never need to know how to run a plantation in Puerto Rico, that gaming activity stimulates pathways of thought that then help the mind respond to a variety of life situations. The same holds true for the social aspect of gaming: While the activity may not seem like something directly applicable to life, it does allow you to improve your social skills so you can be more flexible in real-world situations.

Gaming has also taught me how to analyze a situation for the underlying rules. In many electronic games, not all of the rules of the game are presented up front; players must experiment within the world to learn the rules. Going through these different worlds, scenarios, and rule sets helps me to navigate the many unstated rule sets that govern life.

At the 2007 American Library Association (ALA) midwinter conference, I first saw Dance Dance Revolution (DDR) applied to a library context by Jenny Levine at the ALA TechSource booth. After we danced, we chatted about how libraries are using games. The rest of that show was a blur, as my mind raced about what was happening and what the potential was. I knew there was much more to gaming than teens and DDR, and I had a lifetime of experience to tap to explore it. After several days of contemplation, I decided to change the path of my research to focus on gaming in libraries.

To have a home for my exploration, I created the Library Game Lab of Syracuse as a part of the Information Institute of Syracuse, run by R. David Lankes. The goal of the Library Game Lab is to explore the intersections between gaming and libraries. Our first project was to gather some baseline data to get a better idea of how many libraries were supporting gaming of all types. We randomly selected 400 public libraries and called them to learn how they work with gaming. We also did a census where we put out a call for libraries to tell us more about their gaming programs.

The data from these studies allowed us to pursue funding. Gaylord, a company that provides libraries with supplies, furniture, and archival solutions, provided considerable assistance with a startup grant that allowed us to purchase the games that are most typically used by libraries. This allowed us to build up the portable Game Lab, which we then used to work with groups of librarians to teach them about the variety of gaming experiences. Taking this lab on the road also helped me to better understand the needs and typical questions that library staff who are new to gaming have.

Gaming continued to grow within ALA, but these discussions tended to take place in a number of small channels specific to a type of library or age of patron. I knew a lot of these different groups could learn from speaking to each other, so I started a Members Initiative Group for Games and Gaming at ALA (connect.ala.org/node/66247). This group brings together people from public, school, and academic libraries to talk about all sorts of games. I wanted to capture the same atmosphere with the Games in Libraries podcast (www.gamesinlibraries.org), and many of the people active in the Members Initiative Group are also voices on the podcast.

Two other significant activities by Jenny Levine and Dale Lipschultz at ALA have helped raise awareness of gaming in libraries. The biannual Gaming, Learning, and Libraries Symposium is a chance for hundreds of interested attendees to share ideas, learn about new games, and work together to move thinking about the topic forward. ALA also received a large grant from the Verizon Foundation and Thinkfinity.org to pursue investigations into teens, gaming, and literacy. One great outcome from this grant is the Librarian's Guide to Gaming toolkit (www.librarygamingtoolkit.org).

Throughout these discussions, I've seen many library staff members or volunteers with a passion for a specific game try to create a program around a game and then struggle to find the appropriate place for that game within the services of the library. This issue inspired me to create the model for thinking about games that is used in this book. After creating this model, I wanted to share it, so I got some funding from the Kaufmann Initiative project to build a daylong workshop, which I presented across the state of New York.

This workshop then inspired a monthlong online course for credit through Syracuse University. Rather than teach a password-protected course, I decided to do it through a series of public videos in June 2009, hosting the course discussions with ALA Connect. After creating the videos for the course, I took the main topics, expanded them, and created this book.

My hope is that *Everyone Plays at the Library* will help librarians develop gaming programs that come out of the mission of the library, as well as provide a positive gaming experience for their patrons. A good match between a patron and a game can lead to an experience that changes that patron's engagement with games. Gaming allows libraries to provide a storytelling-like activity for many different groups of patrons, and when they select the game type appropriately, gaming can fully support the library's mission as well.

Whether you have been a gamer for life or haven't played anything since you were forced into a traumatic dodgeball game in high school, this book can help you think about how gaming fits into library services and will guide you through a process that starts with the library mission and ends with the continuous assessment of gaming programs. The content is useful for libraries of all types and patrons of many different age groups. Gaming is not just video games and is not just for teens, so I invite you to enjoy *Everyone Plays at the Library!*

INTRODUCTION TO GAMING IN THE LIBRARY

Part 1 of this book is designed to frame the rest of the work. To start, I present some of the common questions asked about gaming in libraries and how I typically answer those questions. Many of you will be asked these questions as you start exploring gaming programs, and it is useful to have some good answers at hand. I then talk about the differences between games and gaming and introduce the concept of "the gaming experience." Finally, I introduce an original conceptual framework that serves as the basis of organization for how to classify different types of gaming experiences in library settings.

Games and the Library's Mission

A game is a form of play with goals and structure.
—Kevin Maroney, *The Games Journal*

There are many definitions of games presented by scholars of ludology, the study of games. As with any serious pursuit of a topic, the best way to start is to present the definition that will be used for the given work. The definition of a game, for the purposes of this book, is "a form of play with goals and structure."[1] While this is a rather simplistic definition, it captures the breadth of game formats available. This makes it a good fit for gaming in libraries as it matches the breadth of media formats that libraries support.

There are three components to this definition. The first is the concept of *play*, which separates a game from other forms of activities that are game-like but are not play. Professional sports, for example, are not seen by the players as a play activity. Play can have other benefits—games build many different skills and different types of life literacies—but this emphasizes the importance of considering that the gaming activity should be viewed as play. This is where a number of educational "games" fall short, in that they are really drills in a game form and fail at the aspect of providing play. Without the aspect of play, games also lose their motivational power to inform. A game without play is not a game.

The second component is *structure*. A play activity without structure is simply play. The components of a game can be used for play without the rules to manipulate them. The tabletop game Crossbows and Catapults has bricks that can be used to build castles and devices that fling disks across the table to knock down these bricks. Many children (and adults) do not bother with the rules and play with the components of the game as a toy. While this is play, it is not a game until rules are imposed.

These rules, though, do not have to be the official rules that come with a game. The players can develop their own rules to make play into a game, and many times children will do exactly this after mastering the basic concepts of a plaything. A swing, for example, may be used as a toy to rock back and forth; conversely, by adding a start point and rules about how high each swing must be, players can then compete to swing the most number of times in a time period. A sandbox can be used as a place to play, or a game can be created around building the tallest sand castle.

The final component to this definition is the *goal*. Without a goal, a play activity with structure is still just play. The swing game just described is still just swinging if the goal of "highest number of qualifying swings in a time period" is not set. The goal gives the play a purpose, allows players to improve, and sets limits on the activity. The goal is also a critical part of motivation. Goals can be self-imposed to turn play into a game. Goals can also be long-term or short-term; a role-playing game (RPG), for example, does not typically have an overarching goal, but instead, it has many smaller goals that are imposed both by the players and by the game master who runs the game.

Using this definition helps us to consider what falls into the area of a game activity. Jigsaw puzzles, for example, fall into this definition of a game and are used by libraries in a very similar way to other tabletop game activities. Sports and gambling may be games, depending upon the view of the activity as play; professionals are doing the activity for work and thus come to it with a very different perspective than those enjoying the activity as a play activity. Simulations may be games, depending upon the intent of those using them.

One common question is: "Is Second Life a game?" According to this definition of a game, Second Life and other virtual worlds are not games, as they have no goals. Participants can establish a goal for themselves or can create goals within the virtual world, just as children make their own games out of play in a sandbox. Someone in Second Life may decide that the goal is to build the tallest building on his or her island or to accumulate a million Linden dollars; that person has now turned Second Life into a game. The tools within Second Life can also be used to create games for other people to play, but for the purposes of this book, Second Life is not a game.

"What Do Games Have to Do With Books?"

I was part of a group interview at the 2008 American Library Association (ALA) midwinter conference with a reporter from the *New York Times*. She was cynical about the idea of games in libraries and, after hearing about various projects, asked, "What do games have to do with books?" Her question reflects what many think about games in libraries. For librarians, this will be a question that they face from their managers, boards, the local media, and the public: What role does gaming have in the library? To answer this question, there are a few different perspectives to consider.

What Do Games Have to Do With Books?

Libraries are about more than just books. Many libraries fulfill their missions of providing information via a multitude of formats. Public libraries have carried music for decades, and movies are one of the most popular circulating items. As games are now a popular form of recreational media in the marketplace, they should live alongside other forms of popular recreational media at the library. Therefore, the question "What do games have to do with books?" comes from a lack of understanding of the more holistic nature of what libraries do.

Libraries have circulated games for decades. Many libraries have board games and "games in a book" that can be checked out by patrons. School libraries have also circulated games that are related to the curriculum, and the circulation of video games is of growing interest in public and academic libraries. This process of building and circulating a game collection is based upon library policy and, therefore, it is more straightforward than hosting a gaming program within the library.

Gaming programs have been part of library services for a long time. In the 1850s, libraries hosted Chess clubs. Libraries have hosted bridge and Scrabble clubs, integrated games with summer reading and storytime programs, and provided access to computer games as a way to help people learn and become comfortable with computers. Many of the librarians who we surveyed do not view offering Chess or summer reading games as "gaming in the library," but the reality is that libraries have a history of supporting games. The emphasis on gaming is changing in U.S. society as gaming grows as a significant form of entertainment in adult education. To respond to this change, the emphasis on gaming in libraries is also growing.

Even though games have value as a library offering on their own merits, there *are* in fact connections between many games and books. Many games are set in context, and if that context has a connection to books, then the games can be a great inspiration to players to learn more about the context via reading. A game about music can inspire further interest in music just as a game set in a historical context can inspire someone to want to learn more about that time in history. Gaming can provide inspiration for reading and research; libraries have the ability to tap the motivational facet of games to inspire a patron to learn more about a topic area through traditional library services. The implication of this is that the context in which games are placed is important.

What Does Gaming Have to Do With Literacy?

Another question asked about gaming involves what gaming has to do with literacy. There are several different ways to approach this question based upon different concepts of literacy. The narrowest definition of literacy is based upon reading, and some games do require reading to play. Many board games and RPGs have a considerable number of written rules and text on game components. Some video games also incorporate reading as part of the game through scenes that develop the story, descriptions of items picked up in the game, or text-based menu systems. Eli Neiburger, one of the pioneers in video game tournaments for teens in public libraries, recalled that having to choose the Save option from a menu taught his son the basic building blocks of reading at a very early age.[2]

Defining literacy more broadly makes the connection to games much easier to make. When people read, they are interpreting symbols in context and applying a set of rules to determine meaning from those symbols. Writing is the manipulation of those symbols within a context and a set of rules. These rules can be passed on explicitly or observed and developed implicitly. In a broader sense, developing the ability to take a set of symbols, interpret them, and then manipulate them within a context according to rules is developing literacy skills. In this way, games excel in teaching literacy, as each game requires a player to learn a set of rules and symbols and manipulate those symbols in some way.

Another way to look at literacy is to recognize that there are many forms of literacy needed to live in today's world. James Paul Gee, in his highly cited work *What Video Games Have to Teach Us About Learning and Literacy*, presents 36 different learning principles that games teach players. Some of these include risk-taking, identifying with different roles and cultures, problem solving, and developing tacit knowledge through practice. Those who play a variety of games are more resilient to life changes because they have learned to adapt in many different changing situations.

What Does Gaming Have to Do With Information Literacy?

Within the library context, a common use of the term *literacy* means "information literacy," which involves learning about the discovery, selection, and use of appropriate information resources. There are a few research projects developing games that explicitly teach information literacy skills, but, as is typical, these educational "games" sacrifice fun and gameplay for explicit teaching. Too many educational games focus on education over the game and end up not being an enjoyable experience, which can have a negative impact on learning. Some game-show models for information literacy games, though, do take the entertainment aspects of a game show and combine it with the educational aspect of teaching information literacy to create a more motivational gaming and learning experience.

There are several recreational gaming activities that do require information literacy skills. Because of their complexity, typical role-playing games require several books to be able to play, and players must retrieve information throughout the gaming session. Computer-based RPGs also can require this type of activity. Constance Steinkuehler has written a variety of articles about the development of information literacy skills in massive multiplayer online games.[3] To succeed in these types of games, players must do considerable research about the world in which they live. As the companies producing these games provide few information resources, the players of the games create massive databases, guides, and communities of support as they document every aspect of these virtual worlds.

Isn't Gaming Noisy and Disruptive?

Today's libraries *are* noisy and disruptive! Many libraries now have a quiet room for people who need to focus, while the rest of the library buzzes with groups working and talking, people playing and chatting, and customers enjoying the attached library café. Interactive games fit right in alongside an interactive library. That said, most libraries offer gaming programs in meeting rooms or other areas that are not in the middle of the library so that patrons who need quiet can avoid the noise and excitement that goes along with gaming.

What About Violence in Video Games?

Given the graphical nature of some video games, there is concern about the library presenting the violent side of gaming. If libraries are circulating games, then the same policy that dictates the selection of violent movies and violent books should dictate the selection and circulation of violent video games. If the game is being played as a library program, then the library needs to know why that particular game was selected for the program. If there is an underlying goal for the gaming program that can be met only through a violent video game, then the answer to this question comes from that goal. If the goal for the library program can be met through video games without graphic violence, then libraries can make those choices. Just as libraries do not purchase every book that is published, they do not purchase every game that is produced.

What About Gaming Addiction?

The concept of addiction is not applicable just to games—other forms of media such as books, music, or movies can be just as addictive. Consider the large posters in the library with the single word *READ*: Libraries have been "pushing addiction" through reading for decades. Any recreational activity can be addicting; just ask someone who stayed up all night to finish a gripping novel or watch a season's last few episodes of his or her favorite television series. Gaming is no different from these other recreational activities. If a community is concerned about game addiction, the library can run gaming through regularly scheduled short gaming programs instead of having gaming available all of the time.

What Does Gaming Have to Do With the Library?

This brings us to what the real question should be: What does gaming have to do with the library? It is important that gaming support a library's mission. As gaming takes resources away from other library activities, gaming services should be developed within the mission and goals of the library, in balance with other services. While games are fun, the justification that the library is spending resources on games because they are fun is not a reason that will please boards of trustees or upset patrons. Instead, gaming needs to support the library's mission in some way.

From the surveys of libraries done through the Library Game Lab of Syracuse over the last few years, the three most popular goals in bringing gaming programs into the library are: 1) games are used to attract underserved populations, 2) games are an additional service for groups already using the library, and 3) games provide an opportunity for members of a library community to interact socially with each other, improving the library's role as a community hub. For many library users, their interaction with game media has replaced time spent interacting with book, music, and movie media, so providing access to game media is the next logical step for the library. Gaming provides useful marketing tools in getting the attention of those who feel the library has nothing for them and can draw them into the library. Once they get people in the door, libraries can expose users to other library services; therefore, gaming as a marketing tool is one way that gaming can fit into the mission of the library.

Many libraries, regardless of type, have a goal of being a community hub. They are nonbiased, safe, noncommercial spaces where members of the community can interact; this type of space can be difficult to find. The internet has done a good job in allowing people to find communities online, but the result is that there are fewer local communities. The library can provide that type of community hub. Through gaming, it can provide an activity that engages people of different ages and backgrounds who may never meet in social settings elsewhere, but who all live in the same physical space.

It is this aspect of gaming in libraries—gaming across age groups—that is an inspiration for this book. Gaming is a multifaceted activity. There are gaming programs that can be targeted for children, teens, adults, or seniors; however, there are also gaming programs that are appropriate for everyone. Carefully designed gaming programs can reach out to many different age groups and allow members of these groups to meet and engage with each other in a way not possible in most social settings. Games can build bonds between members of a community who would never otherwise meet, such as teens and seniors playing Wii Bowling together, and libraries offer the safe space for this to happen.

Throughout this book, games and gaming programs for each of these audiences—children, teens, adults, seniors, and intergenerational groups—are presented. While this broad spectrum best matches the audience of a public library, those in school and academic libraries can still find value in this book, especially if the library is open to mixers between students, parents, and teachers. Many of the games discussed in this book are appropriate for players of all ages.

Everyone plays at the library!

Endnotes

1. Kevin Maroney, "My Entire Waking Life," www.thegamesjournal.com/articles/MyEntireWakingLife.shtml (accessed January 13, 2010).
2. Eli Neiburger, "The Payoff, Up Close and Personal," in Gaming, Learning, and Libraries Symposium, Jenny Levine (Chair) (July 2007). Symposium conducted by ALA TechSource in Chicago, IL.
3. For example, see Constance Steinkuehler, "Massively Multiplayer Online Gaming as a Constellation of Literacy Practices," *E-Learning* 4, no.3 (2007): 297–318, dx.doi.org/10.2304/elea.2007.4.3.297 (accessed January 13, 2010).

Games Versus Gaming Experiences

Buy it now! The Newest, Latest, Greatest Game for your Xbox 9000 can be yours today! Why play that old Madden 2015 when you can have the new Madden 2016?

The Game Market

The game market is a fickle one. Games are preannounced, preordered (many times with a promotional music disc, special case, plastic figure, or extra in-game item), and marketed and advertised. They are given sneak peeks by gaming publications, released to stores alongside strategy guides and collectible action figures, and reviewed by both commercial reviewers and interested gamers. They are played and then resold at a fraction of the price to the used game market to help fund the player's purchase of the next game. After a few weeks of release, many games are no longer discussed in the game media; their focus is on the next new release. During awards and end-of-year specials, the games get one final hoorah before being relegated to the $19.99 budget title area of shops.

This is no different from the way that movies, music, and even books are marketed. After the flurry of initial announcements and reviews, save for a few exceptions, the item is not heard about again until there is a change in format (such as when a movie is made available in DVD) or when there are awards. Libraries feel this effect of our consumer culture. Public libraries struggle to balance getting access to enough copies of a new and popular release to satisfy user requests against having many copies of materials that are no longer popular and taking up shelf space. Some libraries rent popular titles to aid with this problem, others charge for circulation of new items (which creates tiered service and a barrier to access), and still others create shorter circulation times for new items.

Because of their focus on new releases, savvy gamers expect libraries to have the newest game. It can get very expensive to attempt to meet this demand, given that each copy of a popular console game currently costs about $60, and few discounts are available. The short shelf life of games compared to other forms of media makes it difficult for libraries to be as attractive as their local game shop in providing access to a collection of the newest and most popular circulating titles. Libraries wishing to provide a circulating collection may need to revisit their collection development and weeding policies to create a frequently refreshed collection that their gaming users respect. Revising these policies would also provide a great opportunity to create a focus group of local gamers, engaging them in library policy review. Engaging local users helps give them a sense of ownership of the library and develops a core volunteer group to staff future gaming activities.

Focusing on One Game

Aggressive marketing techniques draw the attention of librarians and library patrons. As I have worked with librarians to help them start gaming programs, I have found some who want to start a program focused on one popular game, such as the newest iteration of Guitar Hero, the ever-popular World of Warcraft, the latest tabletop game, or some other game that their own children have been begging to play. The problem with this focus on a single game is that it can cost the library much more to satisfy this specific desire than it might cost to select less expensive games that meet the same goals. Often, the most popular games are also the most expensive; libraries with small program budgets would be better off making other choices. Because of this focus on specific games, the market for used older games can be quite favorable to a library building a collection. For instance, the newest version of Madden Football with up-to-date team rosters will cost about $60. A version of this same game with almost identical gameplay and a year-old team roster can be purchased for about $20; or if the library requests it from one of their local gamers or game shops, the game might be easy to acquire through a donation. The used sections of many video game stores, such as GameStop, have many great games that are only a year old at very reasonable prices.

Another good example of a problematic focus on a single game is World of Warcraft. This is a popular game that some libraries have used for programs. To provide the full World of Warcraft experience, libraries need to purchase a copy of the game and copies of two expansions for each computer, as well as pay for monthly subscriptions for each computer (or require each participant to have a credit card and set up a trial account to explore the game). The desire to use World of Warcraft, in particular, results in a very expensive program with a single offering; those same funds could be used instead to create a much broader choice of gaming programs, including access to Runescape, Guild Wars, or other less expensive games that provide a similar experience.

This concept of focusing on one game extends beyond video games. Early in my explorations of games and libraries, I worked with a library to start a gaming program. The library asked about what board games it should purchase, and I suggested one of the well-known gateway board games, The Settlers of Catan. I also helped the library run the gaming program and taught the board games. While I knew Settlers well, I also quickly discovered that the 60–90 minutes it took to play a game made it an inappropriate choice for the library's 2-hour time block for a gaming program. Most of the attendees wanted to play shorter games so that they could try a variety of games in the program. By focusing on the game rather than considering the overall gaming experience, my advice cost the library about $40 from its gaming budget for a game that would not be played frequently during its program sessions. Had I asked more questions about the vision for the gaming program, I could have made better suggestions.

The Game Versus the Gaming Experience

To determine what games to purchase, librarians need to focus on the "gaming experience" not on the game. This concept was first presented by James Paul Gee, who discusses the design of games for learning in his chapter in *The Ecology of Games: Connecting Youth, Games, and Learning*. When talking about setting goals for players, he says, "it is precisely here that talking about 'games'—and not 'gaming' as a social practice—falls short. A good deal of reflection and interpretation stems from the social settings and practices within which games are situated."[1] Two pairs of contrasting examples follow.

Scenario No. 1: A library advertises a board game event. When participants arrive, the librarian points to a corner table in the library with well-worn copies of Monopoly, Scrabble, and Risk. Players poke through the games and perhaps select one they already know, sit down with friends they came with, and play the game. Even if the library has newer games like Ticket to Ride, most players would not attempt to read the rules and play a new board game without guidance.

Compare that situation to a facilitated board gaming experience where players enter a room with a number of board games laid out and ready to play. Also at the ready are staff or volunteers to teach the games. A facilitator works to seat people from different groups together and teaches players how to play the game. As the game finishes, the facilitator works to break up groups and help people find new games to play. The gaming experience allows participants to meet each other and try new experiences; it builds the library as a social hub.

Scenario No. 2: A library advertises a video game event. When players arrive, there is a game system or two in a back room. Players can select their game, and they are left alone to enjoy the games with each other. They may or may not take turns, and after a few hours, the library staff returns to make sure everything is there and to close down the program. While gaming is going on in the library building, it's not integrated with library staff and resources.

Compare this situation to a video gaming experience where the library staff members are involved in a video game program that is more in the open. They stay in the space with the games and the players, giving feedback about their performance, providing tips, and playing when needed. They also have other library materials on the topic available for spectators to browse. The attendees have an experience of gaming that is integrated with library staff and resources and aren't hidden away in the back room during the gaming experience.

For libraries running gaming programs, this concept of the gaming experience is critical to good decision making. The gaming experience is much more than just the game; it also involves the social experience between players, between players and observers, between attendees and librarians, and even between attendees and the building and collection of the library. The game is one small piece at the center of all of these interactions, and the focus in planning needs to be from the perspective of the gaming experience—and therefore, more importantly, of the user.

Librarians might find it useful to compare gaming to similar activities, such as storytime. The focus on a storytime session is not on the story itself but rather on the overall storytime experience. The story provides the inspiration for a series of interactions, activities, decorations, and related materials. When planning a storytime activity, libraries start with the larger questions about the purpose of storytime, what type of experience the storytime should include, what age ranges the story should target, how long the storytime should be, and how to evaluate the success of the storytime. Once these larger questions are considered, then the librarian seeks a story that fits these needs. The story selection only comes once these larger questions about the goals of storytime have been answered.

Questions to Consider for the Gaming Experience

When developing a gaming program, librarians should start by answering this question: What is the gaming experience that we wish to provide?

Some aspects to consider are:

- What age groups are we looking to attract with gaming?
- What kind of space do we have available for the gaming program? How noisy can the gaming experience be?
- How long do we want the program to run? Is this to be a one-shot program or one in a sequence?
- What equipment do we already have? How much money do we have to purchase new equipment?
- What other library programs or services would we like to integrate or promote with the gaming program?
- What expertise do we have available, either from staff or from volunteers?
- What is the goal of the gaming program, and how does this fall in line with the goals and policies of the library?

All of these questions point to the larger gaming experience. By first considering these questions and then choosing appropriate games, libraries are much more likely to have a successful gaming program. Following this process also makes the gaming program much easier to justify as the goals and experience are designed based upon the library and available resources.

While this may seem obvious, many libraries don't use this type of procedure. More commonly, an excited librarian gets funding for games and rushes out to purchase a new console or heavily marketed game. The library puts together a program around the game, but then finds that it doesn't have all of the proper equipment needed for that game or staff who know how to run the game. The library may learn that it needs to spend many hours unlocking songs to make the game fully playable, that it has no supporting collection for those wanting to learn more, or that the game is too complex or too easy for the intended audience. All of these traps await librarians who focus on a specific game rather than considering the overall gaming experience.

Games in Collections Versus Gaming in Programs

The distinction between games and gaming experiences aligns with the two ways in which libraries typically interact with games: A collection focuses on the game itself; the gaming program focuses on the gaming experience.

Games in Collections

Libraries that build collections of games for patrons to check out and play at home are focused on the game. Their collection development decisions should come from library policies. Controversy surrounding issues such as violent content in video games can then be handled in the same way that libraries handle violent content in movies or in books: An appropriate set of policies dictating collection boundaries, circulation policies, and reconsideration of materials applies to games just as it applies to other forms of media.

Academic libraries build collections of games for different purposes. Some of them build up a recreational game collection that lives alongside a recreational fiction collection, and these collections are akin to circulating collections in public libraries. More commonly, academic libraries build game collections to support the curriculum. These games may be circulated or may be played in-house, just as users play music or movies at an in-library station. These collections, just as with most other collections in an academic library, are developed according to the needs of the curriculum. In this case, the focus is still on the game but may also include the education that the game can provide for a class.

Special collections of games also live in academic or public libraries (or museums). These collections also focus on the game as an object of study, and the games may be playable by patrons. The focus of these collections is on the game and, more specifically, on the preservation and study of the game. This may also entail the preservation of the game-playing system for a video or computer game. More libraries will find themselves the benefactors of personal game collections as aging gamers bequeath their collections.

In all of these cases, the focus is on the game itself. Librarians building these collections need to avoid the marketing hype and focus on their collection development policies. Just as libraries collect more than one type of book, libraries should consider collecting more than one type of game. While this book focuses on gaming programs in the library, those building game collections will also find value in learning about the variety of game types to ensure their collection is an appropriate representation of the breadth of games available.

Gaming in Programs

Providing an engaging gaming experience is one overarching concern of many library gaming programs. The focus encompasses more than the game itself; it is on the overall experience. From the annual census survey that I've done of libraries, it is clear that the purpose of most library gaming programs is more than simply "playing games in the library." Most libraries state that entertainment is one of the goals of a gaming program, but few claim that entertainment is the primary goal of that gaming program. Instead, the most prevalent goals are to bring people into the library who typically don't use the library, to meet the needs of those who already use the library and are seeking an additional service, and to create a community activity that allows patrons to interact at the library.[2]

Remember, for a library to run a successful gaming program, the staff first need to think about the gaming experience it wants to provide and then select the games that will best bring about that experience. These experiences are usually different from those experiences users can have with the same game in the home environment. Focusing on and marketing these different experiences is what will bring users out of their homes and into the library to engage with others in a shared gaming experience. While at the library, users may change their mind-sets about libraries as they see some of the other experiences that libraries can offer, and they also get to know other members of their local community in a safe, unbiased, and noncommercial space.

Endnotes

1. James Paul Gee, "Learning and Games," in *The Ecology of Games: Connecting Youth, Games, and Learning*, ed. Katie Salen (Cambridge, MA: The MIT Press, 2008), 21–40, doi:10.1162/dmal.9780262693646.021 (accessed January 13, 2010).
2. Scott Nicholson, "Go Back to Start: Gathering Baseline Data about Gaming in Libraries," *Library Review* 58, no.3 (2009): 203–214.

A Conceptual Model of the Library Gaming Experience

When running a gaming program, a library's focus should be on the gaming experience and not on the game itself. For example, there are many different types of board games. The gaming experience brought about by a strategy board game, where people are fairly quiet and engaged in thought, is different from the gaming experience brought about by a party board game, where people are focused on social interaction. When libraries plan a program, it is better to first consider the gaming experiences they want to facilitate and then select the games to match rather than to select the games and then build the program around the games.

It is important to match gaming experiences with the type of players involved. An early step in planning a gaming program should be to think about the users. The nature of the gaming industry and game marketing can lure planners into the trap of building their programs around a specific game. This can create a program that doesn't match the needs of the library and can be hard to justify.

A better approach is to consider what types of users gaming programs should serve in accordance with the library mission and then develop program goals based on that mission. After establishing these goals, the library selects the gaming experiences that the program will facilitate. Only after this step should the library select specific games for the program. The result is a program based on users that is justifiable and that has library goals by which the program can be assessed.

Model of the Library Gaming Experience

To understand the differences between gaming experience archetypes, it is helpful to first explore a model of the library gaming experience. This model brings together participants, spectators, library staff, and resources, and considers the ways in which they interact.

Players—those engaged with each other through an agreed-upon set of rules in pursuit of a specified goal—bring their own external knowledge to the game based on their prior education and experiences. Spectators may be those who aren't intending to play, such as parents or friends, or those who are not actively playing in a game. During the course of an event, players will become spectators and vice versa as people try different games and wait their turn. Library staff can choose their personal level of involvement; they can put out the games and step back, they can be involved in helping players learn games and meet other players, they can chat with spectators, or they can fill in needed positions in a multiplayer game.

For the purposes of this discussion, a few concepts are important to consider. The focus of the gameplay is the representation of the *game state*. In a board game, this game state representation is the board and the pieces, while in a video game, this representation is presented through changing pixels on the screen. Players typically have some type of avatar in the game state, such as a pawn or character, or they may be directly engaged in the game state. Players interact with each other indirectly by manipulating the game state through a set of agreed-upon rules until the end condition is reached and a winner determined.

Most games are placed within a *game world*. The game world is the story in which the gameplay exists. Sometimes the story is not very involved or even needed to play the game, while other times, it is well developed and a critical part of the gameplay. Some games are set in a pre-existing world, either through tie-ins with other forms of media or by being set in a specific historical setting. In other types of games, the players create the game world as they play the game. Players can interact with each other socially in different ways; in some games, players take on the role of characters and interact as their characters, while in other games, players interact as themselves. All of these components are shown together in Figure 3.1.

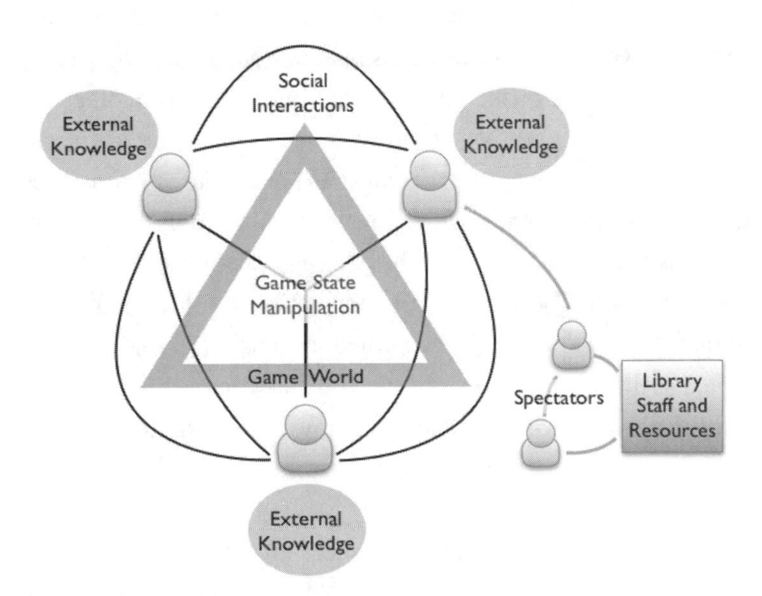

Figure 3.1 Model of the library gaming experience

The connection lines in the model represent interactions. There are two parts to an interaction between the player and the game state. First, the player must decide what action to take; second, the player must successfully carry out that action. Most card and board games emphasize the strategic decision-making aspects of this interaction. On the other hand, most video games focus on the second part of the interaction; the challenge comes in the player being able to aim and shoot quickly or to press a button at the correct time. Some games, such as many real-time strategy games in which a player commands an army in real time, reward both strategic decisions and the skill in manipulating the game state effectively. These different aspects of manipulating a game will be important later in the development of gaming experience archetypes.

Several levels of interaction can go on between players. Through the changing of the game state, players interact with each other. It may not be a deep or meaningful level of interaction, such as when one player moves a piece to capture another player's piece. Another form of interaction is direct interaction, such as negotiation or trade between players under the rules of the game. Social interaction is another type of interaction, and it goes beyond the rules of the game. Players can talk about things not related to the current game state, such as previous turns of the game, other games, or nongaming topics; these interactions, however, are still part of the gaming experience.

Spectators may interact with each other about the game or may interact with each other about nongame topics. Depending upon the game and the setting, it may be appropriate for spectators to interact with the players. After an exciting game, it is common to see players become spectators and talk with others about game concepts, strategy, or skills.

Library staff members and volunteers interact with all attendees by welcoming them to the event, explaining the games, and ensuring that players are playing safely and fairly. Library staff should be actively engaged with spectators, helping them to find open games to join, encouraging them to join the fun, and taking the opportunity to talk about related library services.

The final interaction of note is the interaction between the spectators and other library materials. During a gaming program, libraries should display related library materials in areas in which spectators wait for a chance to play. Libraries should consider resources and game-related displays that provoke questions and discussion. For example, a library could display some books that talk about the benefits of recreational gaming and extract quotes from the books for the display. Good choices would be James Paul Gee's *What Video Games Have to Teach Us About Learning and Literacy,* Steven Johnson's *Everything Bad Is Good for You*, and David Williamson Shaffer's *How Computer Games Help Children Learn.* These items, if displayed cleverly, can aid attendees at the program who did not previously know each other in interacting while waiting to play games.

Gaming Experience Archetypes

There are five elements of the gaming experience model that are important for the development of gaming experience archetypes:

1. The social interactions between players due to the game (Social)
2. The engagement between players and the narrative of the game (Narrative)
3. The actions required by the players in changing the game state (Action)
4. The knowledge that the players bring to the game (Knowledge)
5. The decisions required by the players in changing the game state (Strategy)

These five concepts—Social, Narrative, Action, Knowledge, and Strategy (SNAKS)—are the underlying concepts for gaming experience archetypes and are used as the organizational structure for the next five chapters of this book.

Social

A social gaming experience focuses on the social interactions among players. Many party games are focused on social experiences; in fact, the very concept of a party game stresses the importance of the social component. Many other types of games bring about social experiences that are external to the game; Rock Band, for example, is known for bringing about a social gaming experience. The social gaming experience is most appropriate for a library focusing on creating a community hub through game programs.

Narrative

A narrative gaming experience focuses on activities that interact with the underlying story behind the game. Role-playing games, both face-to-face and online, focus on this concept of narrative as players are interacting within an established world and are helping to tell the story of their character within the world. Other games have a narrative available, but that narrative is optional to the successful playing of the game. A library seeking to offer a narrative gaming experience should focus on those games that have gameplay elements that require players to engage with the story of the game.

Action

An action gaming experience focuses on the player's ability to make changes in the game state. Most video games facilitate action gaming experiences; once a player decides what to accomplish in the game, a challenge comes in actually executing that decision in a timely fashion. Tabletop games that incorporate a dexterity element, such as Jenga, create an action gaming experience. These experiences can be frustrating to participants without experience when they play against those who are more experienced.

Knowledge

A knowledge gaming experience focuses on aspects of the world that are usually external to the game itself. Most educational games fall into this category, as do some party games. Some of these games are designed to help players gain and then demonstrate knowledge, while others allow players to demonstrate previously acquired knowledge. Libraries concerned about the acceptance of gaming programs can start with knowledge gaming experiences, as these experiences tend to easily fit within the educational mission of most libraries.

Strategy

A strategy gaming experience focuses on the intellectual aspects of the decision making required to play a game. These decisions include both the short-term tactical decisions required to take advantage of the current game stage and the long-term strategic planning needed to guide a player's actions over the course of a game. Strategy gaming experiences tend to be longer and more serious games that create a subdued environment, which might be what a library with limited space needs to focus on.

In the next five chapters, these gaming experience archetypes will be more fully explored. Different gaming experiences are appropriate for different library goals and patron demographics. Specific game titles can facilitate more than one gaming experience; for example, the aforementioned Rock Band can be used for both social and action gaming experiences. Libraries will need to decide if they want a gaming program built around one type of gaming experience that focuses on a single group and purpose or one that has a variety of gaming experiences to provide a broader gaming program to reach out more widely.

Part 2

The Five Gaming Experience Archetypes

The next five chapters explore each of the five gaming archetypes. Within each chapter is a discussion of the various types of games that can facilitate each archetype. Specific game titles are discussed within the context of the archetype, which goes against the traditional format-based method of organizing games; this is in order to discuss board and video games together. The focus is not on the game itself but how games can be integrated into a library program and how different types of gaming experiences can meet different library goals.

As this book is focused on gaming in library programs, the focus is also on multiplayer games. There are many single-player gaming experiences, most of which are digital games. Much of the power that games can have is lost when all you do is bring a group of people together just to have them all sit at individual screens and play single-player games, without some type of a larger social context. Therefore, the recommendation is that gaming programs in libraries focus on multiplayer gaming experiences.

These chapters cover a number of game profiles. These profiles are different from typical game reviews that focus on the story and the gameplay elements or that evaluate the game; if the game is listed in a profile, it should be considered as a recommendation. These profiles focus on variables important to a librarian in deciding if a game is appropriate for the library.

Here is the structure of each game profile:

Game name, type of game, publisher, retail price, number of players
Experience: A short synopsis of the game experience from the player's perspective
Demographic: Whether the game is appropriate for child, teen, adult, senior, or all audiences (*Author's Note*: This is a generalization)
Complexity: How complex the game is to teach
Minimum Length: How long one round of the game takes to play
Interaction: What types of interactions exist between players in this game
Skills: Most significant skills that are developed when playing this game (e.g., there are some skills like reading and mathematics that are developed in many games; the purpose here is to list only the most important skills that I perceive are developed in the game)

Here is an example for my own game:

Tulipmania 1637, JKLM Games, $28
Experience: Players manipulate a turbulent stock market and cash out before the crash.
Demographic: Adult
Complexity: Medium
Minimum Length: 30 minutes
Interaction: Manipulation, bidding

Skills: Mathematics, long-term planning, prediction of actions

These reviews should provide a library with enough information to know if a game is worth further consideration for a specific program. The goal is not to provide a catalog of game reviews but to supplement the text with a few selected examples of games; there are many more games in each category that may suffice. Commonly known games such as Chess, Charades, Scrabble, and Monopoly are not reviewed.

For additional information, consult the BoardGameGeek (www.boardgamegeek.com) database, which has become the primary hub for board game hobbyists. In addition, I have created a series of more than 60 free videos where I teach about these games at Board Games With Scott (www.boardgameswithscott.com).

Knowledge Gaming Experiences

Knowledge gaming experiences are those experiences that focus on the knowledge from the external world that a player brings to a game. These games can range from educational games used in a classroom to party games such as the popular Trivial Pursuit in which players recall obscure facts to word games such as Scrabble and Boggle. Many video and computer games also allow players to explore their knowledge, the most common of which are game-show format trivia games. In addition, many big games (in which the players are the pieces and the game is set in the surrounding environment), such as puzzle hunts, provide a knowledge gaming experience.

Knowledge gaming experiences are appropriate for players who enjoy exploring and demonstrating their own knowledge or are interested in learning more. In a school setting, for example, a knowledge gaming experience would be perfect for a gifted and talented class. In a public library setting, these games will be a draw for patrons for whom education has been an important part of their lives. Conversely, these games can exclude many who do not currently or did not care for school and feel that these games are just reliving that experience. Within a school setting, these games can come across as forms of schoolwork and so they may not be appropriate for a recreational program. Other types of knowledge gaming experiences that focus on subtopics such as film or popular culture will draw those who know these topics and want to test their knowledge, and will drive away those who are not engaged with popular culture. Knowledge gaming experiences will inevitably draw in some patrons and drive away others, so it is important to match up knowledge game selections with the interest areas of patrons.

Environment

There are two main environments for knowledge games. The first is a quiet environment, as with games such as Scrabble that involve deep thought. External noise can be a distraction to players of such games. A library with limited space that has to be shared with nongaming library patrons, such as a school library or one-room public library, can consider these quieter knowledge gaming experiences.

The second environment is a game-show environment for party-style knowledge games, where players are laughing, working together, and engaging socially. With this type of knowledge game, the game needs to be played in a space away from normal library use, as these games can generate considerable excitement. This environment can easily draw an audience, as people are drawn to watching game shows.

Knowledge games can work in a team environment quite well, especially if teammates are allowed to consult about an answer. Many knowledge games place players on teams. A library seeking an activity that groups can do together should consider a knowledge gaming experience.

Educational Games

Most educational games are focused more on education and less on the game. These games typically mimic school-like experiences, such as drills or exams, with some type of a light gaming experience wrapped around them. This is true for both analog and digital games; in some cases, the analog board game model of roll a die, move, and answer a question is mapped directly into the digital space. Some games develop a more in-depth story or use flashy graphics, but at the core, the player is answering questions about educational topics to get a reward.

School libraries have supported classroom needs with educational games for decades. The *Standard Library Organization and Equipment for Secondary Schools of Different Sizes* guide, published by the American Library Association (ALA) in 1920, briefly discusses games as one of the resources that school libraries should include. As computers came in to school libraries, librarians became engaged with computer-based educational games.

Brian Mayer and Chris Harris focus on the concept of "authentic games" for school libraries, looking at board games produced for recreational purposes and analyzing what learning standards these games apply to. Their recent ALA title, *Libraries Got Game: Aligned Learning Through Modern Board Games*, thoroughly explores this concept and recommends many games for school librarians. The future is encouraging for educational games as they continue to improve, moving away from the quiz model toward games that teach through the interactions between players and game elements and players with each other.

Given the range of purposes for educational games as a teaching tool, an exploration of these games is outside the scope of this book. The focus of this book is on recreational games, many of which can be used for educational purposes, so games created for purely educational purposes are not discussed. Instead, the focus is on recreational games and what those games can teach.

Game Show, Trivia, and Party Games

Game shows in the U.S. started on radio and continue to be popular on television. One reason for this popularity is that viewers can relate to the contests on the shows, as the contestants are everyday people. Viewers can play along with the show and see how they would perform in the same situation. There was a game show scandal in the late 1950s in which producers were found to have given answers to contestants and rigged shows so that popular contestants would continue to win—all to attract more viewers. As a result, additional controls were placed on these shows. After a brief hiatus, game shows returned and flourished as popular sources of entertainment.

Over the decades, game shows have inspired board games. In fact, a long-standing prize for many shows is a copy of the board game to play at home. The first edition of the board game Password sold more than 2 million copies when it was released in 1962; as a point of comparison, it took Scrabble three years to sell 1 million games.[1] These games are popular because they allow players to have the experience of the game show at home. Games based on game shows can be very popular in libraries, either as games for small groups or as games with an audience, where players are selected from the audience to come up and play, perhaps for a real prize. Most of these games are focused on trivia or external knowledge (such as obscure connections between concepts in Password).

Games fashioned after game shows inspired other similar games not connected to television shows. Many of these trivia games share the same problem as educational games: The focus of the game is on asking players questions, with little focus on any other aspects of gameplay. Without other clues, the questions can't be figured out; either the player knows the answer or sits in silence attempting to think of something to say.

Trivial Pursuit was an extremely popular game in the 1980s that used the model of rolling a die, moving on a track, and answering questions. The popularity of this game spawned many clones, and the model of a trivia game was born in the modern gaming mind-set. Over the last few years, there have been some changes. Wits and Wagers is a game I refer to as "Trivial Pursuit 2.0." Much as Web 2.0 is about adding interaction, Wits and Wagers brings about a much more social experience in that all players answer a question at the same time, and then players bet on whose answer is best. Wits and Wagers rewards knowledge, social experience, and game strategy. This model is now inspiring new approaches to trivia games. The game Triviathon, for example, presents players with four choices; players pick one choice each, and their answer dictates how far they move. (See Figure 4.1 for an example card.)

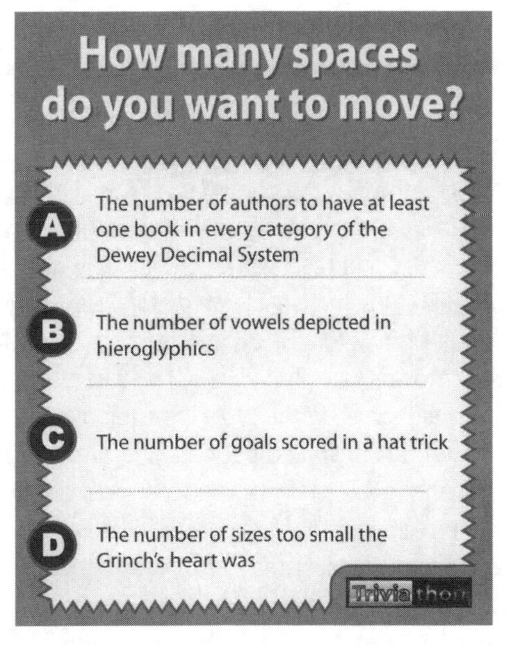

Figure 4.1 Sample card from Triviathon (Reprinted with permission of Jeezle Pete's!)

Party games, similar to Password, focus on external knowledge but not necessarily trivia. A long-standing party game in this category is Charades. In fact, a library could use a game of Charades and combine it with a book talk, where teams act out the title of a book, and then the librarian talks about what the book is about. One of the more popular commercial games in this category in the last few decades is Pictionary, where players take turns drawing pictures of objects for their team to guess. From the popularity of Pictionary came Cranium, where players not only draw but also act, sing, sculpt, and answer trivia questions. The creators of Cranium have continued to create a line of party games that tap into different types of external knowledge over the years. One of the best is the out-of-print Cranium Hoopla, which has the players working together cooperatively on one team against "the game," represented by a timer.

The Georgetown (SC) County Library, through the BYTES Project and a special Hurricane grant, hosted weekly Disaster Game Nights over the summer of 2009. On Disaster Game Nights, area youth competed to get the high score in the Stop Disasters game (www.stopdisastersgame.org/en/home.html), which is a browser-based computer game created by the UN/ISDR (United Nations/International Strategy for Disaster Reduction). Players took on the role of city planners in an effort to prepare their towns for hurricanes, wildfires, earthquakes, floods, and tsunamis. In the Stop Disasters game, the youth had to contend with limited budgets and time constraints to meet scenario goals such as educating local citizens and alerting them to imminent disasters, creating safe housing for locals, and defending the resources that create a viable local economy.

We had between 12 and 27 youth participate weekly, learning not only how deadly these disasters can be but also how individuals and communities can better prepare to survive them.

Donald Dennis,
Georgetown County Library System

A recent advance in party games is the conversion of board games into stand-alone electronic party games. These battery-operated toys contain the questions, time the game, and keep score. Some of them are completely self-contained, such as Catch Phrase and Guesstures. These games are good for library settings because there are no pieces to lose, and they take up much less space than the full board game. The disadvantage is that the library needs to have spare batteries on hand.

There are digital versions of these games for computers and consoles as well. The most common are versions of game shows; digital versions of Jeopardy and Wheel of Fortune have been produced for many computer and console platforms, and licensed digital versions of trivia board games exist as well. In fact, there was an arcade version of Trivial Pursuit in the 1980s. This type of game is popular today in bar-top game consoles and ties in well with other trivia games popular in some pubs. Some digital games are also styled after the game show model, one of the best being the You Don't Know Jack series of games popular in the late 1990s. One of the strongest current franchises of this model of game is Buzz!, which comes with specialized controllers that light up and a smarmy game show host.

Wits and Wagers, board game, North Star Games, $29.99, 4–21 players
Experience: Players answer numerical questions simultaneously, then wager on which player is closest to the real answer.
Demographic: All (mixed teams work well)

Complexity: Low
Minimum Length: 5 minutes for one round (a full game is seven rounds)
Interaction: As players wager on each other's answer, they first mentally interact; then after the answer is read, they socially interact.
Skills: Knowledge, probability/odds, determining strengths of others

Triviathon, board game, Jeezle Pete's, $29.99, 2–12 players
Experience: In this trivia game, players answer multiple-choice questions, each choice with a different reward.
Demographic: All (mixed teams work well)
Complexity: Low
Minimum Length: 45 minutes, although players can drop out and join in during the game
Interaction: Very little required. Each player has a special ability, which adds some unusual interactions that may not be appropriate (such as arm-wrestling).
Skills: Knowledge

Electronic Catch Phrase, board game, Hasbro, $29.99, 4+ players
Experience: Two teams take turns trying to get their teammates to say a word or phrase while a random timer ticks toward the end of the round.
Demographic: Teens, adults, seniors who are accepting of time pressure
Complexity: Low
Minimum Length: 2–3 minutes for one round
Interaction: Considerable discussion and interaction between team members
Skills: Knowledge, communication, thinking under pressure

Buzz! series, console game, Sony, $40–$60 (depending on version), 1–8 players

Experience: This game show experience for up to 8 players (with 2 copies) comes complete with flashing lights, smarmy host, and lots of noise and excitement.
Demographic: Teens, adults
Complexity: Low
Minimum Length: 5 minutes for one round. Different game modes have different numbers of rounds.
Interaction: Low between players, although the final round has players selecting others to knock out of the game
Skills: Knowledge, thinking under pressure

Word Games

When thinking of word games, most people think of Scrabble. Scrabble is the Chess of the knowledge game category, with the National Scrabble Association organizing tournament play through clubs across the country. In fact, one easy way for a library to attract players is to host a Scrabble tournament; by requesting that players bring their own boards, this tournament can be run very inexpensively. A local Scrabble club may be interested in running the tournament for the library, thus reducing staff costs. Many libraries already have Scrabble boards, so this is a form of gaming that may already be available.

There are word games other than Scrabble. Hangman is the first word game that most people learn to play and still can be a fun activity. It also can be a very low-cost but quite competitive library program. The concept of Hangman was expanded and made popular with the Wheel of Fortune game show. Bananagrams is a spelling game similar to Scrabble but with simultaneous play and no board. My Word! is a fast-paced card game where players call out words when they see them in a jumbled mess of letters on a table.

Boggle is a word game that can be played more quickly than Scrabble (and, with a video camera and a projector, can be used with an entire room of players at the same time). Password is a different type of word game that focuses on the connections between words rather than on the construction and spelling of the words, while the party game Balderdash is based on a classic parlor game called Dictionary where each player writes a fake definition of a word. The fake definitions are mixed up with the real definition, and players try to guess which is the real one. The new party game Word on the Street has two teams spelling words to capture letters in a combination word and strategy game.

Because of the connection between words and reading, word games are a natural fit for libraries wanting to promote literacy through gaming. Word-based games can be an easily justifiable place to start a library gaming program when libraries face a skeptical board or patron group.

Bananagrams, Bananagrams, LLC., $14.99, 2–8 players
Experience: Players work simultaneously to use all of their letters in crossing words in front of them.
Demographic: All, although children may need fewer letters
Complexity: Low
Minimum Length: 20 minutes per round
Interaction: None, since players work on their own
Skills: Word exploration, thinking under pressure

My Word!, Out of the Box, $9.99, 2–6 players
Experience: Letter cards are flipped up one by one. Players call out words and grab the letters.
Demographic: All
Complexity: Low
Minimum Length: 10 minutes per round

Interaction: Very little
Skills: Word exploration, thinking pressure

Word on the Street, Out of the Box, $24.99, 2+ players
Experience: Two teams come up with a word to match a category. Teams slide letter tiles used in spelling that word toward their side of the board in an attempt to remove eight tiles from the board.
Demographic: All (mixed teams work well)
Complexity: Low
Minimum Length: 30 minutes, although players can join and leave teams during the game
Interaction: Members of a team have to agree upon the word to use. The other team may heckle them by offering "helpful" suggestions.
Skills: Word exploration, teamwork

Big Games

The concept of big games covers a wide spectrum of game types. Big games are typically not commercially available games but instead are put together by staff for a specific setting. The basic concept of big games is that the game board is the real world and the players are the game pieces. These life-sized games can handle large numbers of players. Reality television shows such as *Survivor* and *The Amazing Race* are examples of big games. Some of the games already described could be the inspiration for big games, such as playing Charades or Hangman in a large room for everyone to play at once. Another type of big game that supports a knowledge gaming experience is a puzzle hunt. In these games, players solve puzzles that unlock hints to the location of the next set of puzzles. This combines a treasure hunt with working through puzzles and can be a great team experience. It is also a good type of game to tie into a specific book or author for a themed puzzle hunt.

A global positioning system (GPS) can be used for a form of big game known as geocaching. In geocaching, players are given a location and use the GPS device to navigate to that area. Once players arrive at the area, they are given a riddle or a clue as to the exact location of the reward. The cache is a box or container, and once the players find it, they record information about themselves in a log book, take one of the trinkets in the box, and leave their own trinket behind. Geocaches around the world have been registered at Geocaching.com (www.geocaching.com), and libraries could easily build a program that teaches participants how to use a GPS device, pointing them to nearby caches, placing some of their own caches, and registering them at Geocaching.com.

Another form of big game that can provide a knowledge gaming experience is an alternate reality game (ARG). In ARGs, a story that is presented to the players is overlaid on the real world, and players must unravel the story as they work through puzzles and challenges. One academic library created an ARG called Blood on the Stacks (www.trinity.edu/jdonald/bloodonthestacks.html), where teams of players investigated the library for clues to a missing artifact. The suspects were the library staff members, and players received a dossier on each (which had the added benefit of letting players get to know different staff members). Players solved puzzles and developed information literacy skills as they explored the mystery to determine who was the culprit.

This ARG model of a big game is a valuable idea for libraries. It allows them to create a facilitated experience that exposes players to a variety of types of library resources and staff members. However, ARGs should involve more than the educational game model of asking a series of questions that people have to look up; the puzzles and activities need to be integrated into the gameplay so that the research is just one aspect of what players are doing. ARGs can be created as stand-alone activities that players can work through on their own time when they want to learn about the library, or they can be part of a larger special event where players are all engaged with the activity at the same time. This type of model can either supplement or replace traditional information literacy classes.

Libraries can combine the excitement of a big game with a game show by running a life-sized version of a game show using a play-at-home game. Trainers Warehouse (www.trainerswarehouse.com) sells a number of components such as question boards, buzzer systems, and spinning wheels that can be used by libraries to create a game show environment for a large community event. There are also both licensed and unlicensed computer-based versions of popular game shows that librarians could use to moderate a similar event, but the clanking of an actual wheel is much more exciting than watching a virtual wheel spin on a projector. Another clever (but expensive) game is Classroom Jeopardy, where someone puts in a series of questions ahead of time. The unit hooks to a television, has buzzers, and keeps score. These customized game shows are great events to tie into an existing library program as the questions can come from a book, a speaker's topic, or a special event in the community.

The University of Dubuque (IA) provides library orientation to incoming football student athletes through Fantasy Football. For the initial program, just over 70 students were asked to help determine the top running back for the season. Through the game of Fantasy Football, students were introduced to the concepts of information literacy. The students discussed various topics including authority, timeliness, accuracy, and relevance to draw conclusions about the top player. After the session, students were asked to provide a written evaluation and to name three criteria for evaluation. Eighty percent of the students named 2 of the 3 criteria correctly.

Paul Waelchli,
Todd Wehr Library, St. Norbert College

Demographics

Children

In conjunction with classroom work, knowledge games can provide an additional way of exploring a topic and, therefore, are a good match for a school library. Some knowledge games that focus more on the fun of the game than on the underlying knowledge will be appropriate for children, especially if the game focuses on trivia that comes from the world of children. A game such as the SpongeBob SquarePants Fact or Fishy DVD Game can be wildly popular with children who love SpongeBob but could be a disaster for children who don't watch the show.

Teenagers

Of all the age groups, teenagers are the least drawn to knowledge gaming experiences. Many knowledge games put players on the spot to demonstrate their knowledge, and this can be a sensitive area for teens. The exception would be a topical knowledge game on a topic known to be popular among a specific group of teens, such as Harry Potter. Another exception would be a gifted group or another group of teens that enjoys demonstrating and testing their knowledge.

Adults

Knowledge games work well with many adult library visitors. Those adults who choose to come to the library are likely to enjoy an experience that develops their knowledge. As always, matching the type of game to the patron is important. Adults are less affected by giving a wrong answer when put on the spot than teenagers, so question-and-answer trivia games can work well. Adults also enjoy the party-style knowledge games like Password, as these games focus on the social side of knowledge.

Seniors

Knowledge games for seniors must be selected carefully. Many knowledge games incorporate quite a bit of popular culture, and this can be frustrating to a senior who isn't part of that culture. A number of knowledge games use time elements that require quick thinking, and this too can be frustrating; in some of these games, the time element can be removed to allow the game to proceed at a more casual pace. Knowledge games that don't rely upon popular culture or time constraints can be great choices to help seniors keep their minds sharp.

Intergenerational

Knowledge gaming experiences are one of the best choices for intergenerational library programs. As most knowledge games span a wide variety of topic areas, these games can be played by intergenerational teams or families. Each member of the team can help fill in the knowledge gaps of the others. Through a shared experience, each of the team members will gain appreciation for the knowledge that others bring to the table.

Library Goals

A knowledge gaming experience makes sense in a library situation where education is important. School libraries can turn to knowledge gaming experiences when they wish to support classroom experiences. Knowledge games resemble the way that many courses are assessed in schools; they are forms of interactive exams. Many educational games are focused more on education than on the game, but there are some exceptions.

Another opportunity for these types of gaming experiences is a topical game event. For example, in line with an Everybody Reads program, a library could put together knowledge gaming experiences that explore topics discussed in the book. In many games, once library staff understand the question structure, they can craft new questions that work with the structure and components of the game. If a town has a special event in line with a famous person or particular occasion, a knowledge gaming experience focused on that event can be a great match. A game featuring knowledge about a specific area can be great for a library event where notable members of the community are invited to play in a game-show format to test their knowledge of the areas.

Knowledge games can be good matches for family game activities, especially if families are placed on teams. Many knowledge gaming experiences have a variety of topics from different time periods, so an intergenerational team can work together to see who knows the answers. This can be a chance for family members to learn and appreciate what each member can bring to a game table.

Endnotes

1. Password, BoardGameGeek, www.boardgamegeek.com/boardgame/1549 (accessed January 13, 2010).

five

STRATEGY GAMING EXPERIENCES

The strategy gaming experience focuses on the meaningful decision-making process that players go through during a game. Most games require decision making to some extent, but elements in the game such as time or chance reduce the emphasis on this decision making. The term *strategy* is used in this book for the general concept of decision making at all levels in a game. Those seriously into games distinguish two types of decision making in a game: strategy and tactics. Strategic planning refers to the long-term planning in a game, while tactics are the short-term decisions needed to decide what to do (usually heading toward a longer-term strategy). These two concepts are grouped into the larger concept of strategy for the purposes of this book.

Out of all of the game types, the oldest example of gaming in U.S. libraries that I have been able to find is a strategy gaming experience through abstract games. (An abstract strategy game is a game with very little luck, no hidden information, and very little narrative, such as Tic-Tac-Toe, Checkers, Chess, or Go.) In 1854, the Mechanics'

Institute library in San Francisco was built with a Chess room. The oldest U.S. Chess club still in existence started in this room.[1] Many libraries already have Chess boards; people engaging each other over Chess is one example of a strategy gaming experience that has a long history in libraries.

Environment

Strategy gaming experiences are typically quiet as players are thinking during their turns. There can be moments of noisy reaction when someone makes a devastating move, but the typical snapshot of the game shows one player deep in thought while others observe and wait their turn. Even multiplayer digital strategy games will usually be fairly quiet, with the exception of a team-based game that can be quite noisy as team members communicate. Having players wear headphones to link them to their teammates can help.

Most of these games are best played by individuals or with individuals playing specific roles on a team. Forcing a group to agree upon a strategic decision for a single game avatar to take can be a very frustrating experience; typically, one team member will take over the decision making and the others will offer advice. If developing the skill of teamwork is part of the goal of playing the game, then using a strategy game with teams instead of individuals can be a great way to hone that skill.

Because of their complexity, many strategy games can take hours to play. Libraries using strategy games need to be aware of the length of individual games and allow enough time for players to learn and enjoy the games. Using strategy games in a tournament setting can require a significant amount of time; a library wishing to run a Chess tournament will probably require all day to do so. Therefore, an important part of preparing the environment for a strategy gaming experience is to allow more time for the gaming program or develop a way to allow players to record their game state to continue it at the next program.

Abstract Strategy Games

Abstract board games have been a leisure pastime for thousands of years. This form of tabletop gaming has been played since at least 2500 BC as documented on wall paintings in ancient Egypt.[2] The game depicted in the wall paintings, Senet, is just one example of many traditional abstract games, such as Go, Nine Men's Morris, Mancala, Parcheesi, Checkers/Draughts, Backgammon, and Chess, that are still enjoyed today. Most households have a Chess or Checkers set, and many schools and libraries have Chess boards available for play.

Many communities already have Chess clubs, and the members of these clubs can be a great resource for libraries to tap. People in these organizations are passionate about their game and may be willing to partner with the library to start a series of educational Chess programs, a regular Chess club, or Chess tournaments. The U.S. Chess Federation's website (www.uschess.org) lists local Chess clubs. Some communities have similar organizations that support other abstract games like Go or Backgammon. A new organization for two-player abstract games called the International Abstract Games Organization (IAGO; www.abstractgamers.org) is interested in working with libraries and helping individuals find places to play.

The challenge with incorporating two-player abstract strategy games into some library gaming experiences is that not much socialization goes on during a serious two-player game. While one player is thinking, he or she doesn't want to be distracted by the other player talking. These games are usually very quiet, and any social interaction goes on before and after the game itself. A tournament structure can improve interaction, as there will be times when players are not scheduled in matches and can interact with each other. Libraries looking to improve social interactions between participants, though, may want to choose a different type of gaming experience.

Not all abstract games are hundreds of years old; there has been continued development in the two-player abstract games arena. Many of us have played Connect 4 as children, so some of the concepts of modern abstracts are easy to draw back to that experience. Pente is a popular game about capturing and connecting stones that is similar to the classic Go-Moku. A series of six games called the Gipf series renewed considerable interest in two-player abstracts. This series is designed with ways to let players who own several of the games to bring them together, so that they could stop playing one game to play a different game; the winner of the second game has an advantage in the original game. Another game that has grown in popularity is called Hive, which is a tile-based abstract game that has no board; individuals can play this game anywhere with a flat surface. Every year, a number of new two-player abstract games enter the market, but most of these games do not catch on like Gipf and Hive. These games tend to be faster than traditional abstract games and work well with a wide variety of players. They also are easier to learn than Chess, so new players are engaged more quickly in the gaming experience.

Gipf, board game, Rio Grande Games, $32.95, 2 players
Experience: Players attempt to get pieces in a row, but the better they do, the harder it is to win.
Demographic: All
Complexity: Low
Minimum Length: 20 minutes

Interaction: Piece-based
Skills: Strategic planning

Hive, board game, Gen Four Two Games, $30, 2 players
Experience: Two players control a set of insects, each with special moves, on a boardless space.
Demographic: Teens, adults, seniors
Complexity: Medium
Minimum Length: 20 minutes
Interaction: Piece-based
Skills: Strategic planning

Mechanics-Based Board Games

In the U.S., the mass market board game space is controlled by two companies: Hasbro and Mattel. Hasbro owns a number of well-known board game subsidiaries, including Parker Brothers and Milton Bradley. Over the decades, many board games have been produced with the same model as the first board games: Players move along a track based upon some randomization method, and some spaces have special effects. The prevalence of this model has shaped many American's mental model of what a board game is. These large companies have not traditionally taken risks on their board game design, so well-known games continue to be produced. This has given some of these games a "timeless" nature and has the advantage of creating a large number of players who know how to play games, as is the case with Monopoly and Clue. The disadvantage is that most of these games have significant problems that can create experiences that turn people off of board games, such as the elimination of players or the heavy influence of luck.

This has not been the case in Europe, specifically, in Germany. Over the last few decades, board game development overseas has continued, and well-known companies such as Ravensburger continue to try out new game designs. In the 1990s, a number of these designs made their way over to the U.S. through specialty game publishers and are slowly becoming well-known. The Settlers of Catan is one of the better known games from this development. These games tend to be shorter with fixed ending times, more player interaction, and less dependence on luck. These types of games are commonly known as *Eurogames*, even though they are created all around the world; the terms *designer board games* or *family strategy games* are also used to describe this type of game.

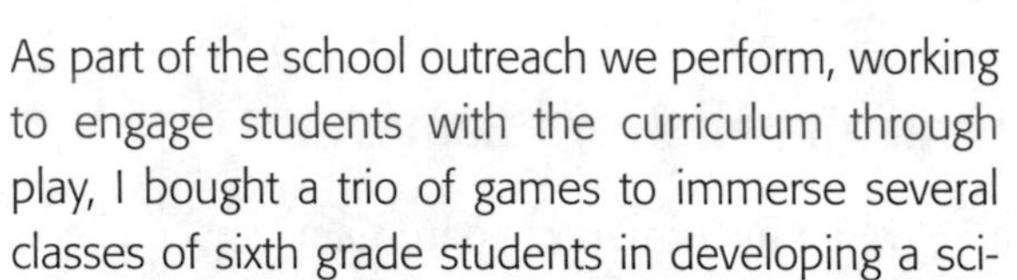

As part of the school outreach we perform, working to engage students with the curriculum through play, I bought a trio of games to immerse several classes of sixth grade students in developing a scientific mind-set in preparation for discussions on the scientific method. Students played Suitcase Detectives by HABA, Zendo by Looney Labs, and Fauna by Huch & Friends over the course of two days. Throughout this period, students strengthened core scientific skills such as induction, deduction, inquiry, and educated guessing in a flexible and challenging environment. Perhaps the greatest success was the eagerness of the students to revisit the resources in the library independently after the program had finished.

Brian Mayer,
School Library System,
Genesee Valley (NY) Educational Partnership

There are two significant elements to many of these games: mechanics and theme. In this section, the focus will be on those games that emphasize the mechanics of the game: the methods by which players interact with the game and with each other. The theme of the game refers to the backstory, the roles that the players take, and how they interact to tell a story. Board games that emphasize the theme are discussed in the narrative gaming experiences chapter.

At the core of many of these games is the concept of resource management. Players have a finite number of resources—turns, cards, money, units—and must use them efficiently to meet game goals. Many of these games offer multiple paths to achieve points, so players must balance risk and reward. This balance is presented in ways that include allowing players to spend a few resources for a few points in a quick move or providing ways for players to get many more points for more resources or more game turns.

Here are some of the mechanics explored in board games:

- In *area control games*, the board is broken up into many different areas with different scoring values. Players spend resources in an attempt to control different areas and must balance their resource supply with the rewards available. Some of these games have ways for players to attack the areas held by others in order to reduce those players' awards. Examples include El Grande and China.

- *Trading games* encourage players to negotiate and to exchange resources with each other. These games create significant opportunity for interaction between players but can be won more easily by someone who is better at negotiation. Examples include The Settlers of Catan and Chinatown.

- *Stock market games* allow players to invest in shares that then rise and fall in value. These games have continued to be popular ever since the classic Acquire. My own game, Tulipmania 1637, is a stock market game that models a bubble market and was inspired by the great tulip bubble in The Netherlands.

- In *auction games*, players try to outbid each other to make the best deals, given limited resources. These games give an advantage to those who know how to read their opponents and push them to their bidding limits. Medici and Modern Art are both older games that embody the auction mechanism.
- In *role selection games*, players have the option to take on roles that give them special abilities. Players must then use their powers in that role to take advantage of the game situation. Puerto Rico is one of the most well-known games focused on a role selection element. Citadels is a lighter card game that mixes role selection with elements of direct conflict.
- In *worker placement games*, the player controls a number of pieces. Each piece goes somewhere on the board to claim an ability, collect resources, or use resources. Caylus is a well-known strategic game that uses worker placement to build a city. Stone Age is a shorter worker placement game about cavemen.
- Rummy is a traditional *set collection game*, and many board games focus on the action of collecting sets of things that will score in different ways. Ticket to Ride is a good family game that focuses on this mechanic, and Ra takes set collection concepts and pairs it with an auction mechanic.
- In *tile placement games,* players are given tiles with different types of paths or buildings and assemble them into high-scoring combinations. Carcassonne is one of the classic tile-placement games that has many variants. Carcassonne: The Discovery is a variant designed for new players to the series. A different type of tile game is Quirkle, which is similar to Scrabble but uses colors and symbols instead of words.
- In *route planning games*, players attempt to determine the most efficient connections between places on the board, given

their resources. A classic game about route planning is the Empire Builder series, where players draw with crayons on the board to make train routes. The aforementioned Ticket to Ride takes the set collection mechanic and pairs it with route planning.

- While most games have some type of element where a player must take risks, *risk-taking games* focus on pressing one's luck. Can't Stop is the best-known of these games, where players roll dice in an attempt to claim number combinations before their opponents do. Incan Gold is a light risk-taking game where players venture into a temple to get the most treasure.
- In order to win *puzzle games*, players must solve a puzzle. In many of these games, such as Ubongo or Take It Easy, players all have similar components and are attempting to solve a puzzle in the most efficient manner. In some games, time is a factor as the players race to be the first one done, and in others, players are not timed but are scored on how well they complete their puzzles.

There are many other mechanics used in these games, and most games combine two or more mechanics. As players become comfortable with these games, it is easier to discuss them by what the mechanics of the game involve. For example, Power Grid, an excellent but longer game about supplying power to cities, combines auctions, a market, and route planning into an interesting economic experience.

Settlers of Catan, board game, Mayfair Games, $42, 3–4 players
Experience: Players trade resources and build infrastructures to produce more resources.

Demographic: Teens, adults, seniors
Complexity: Medium
Minimum Length: 45–60 minutes
Interaction: Trading
Skills: Planning, negotiating, probability

Ticket to Ride, board game, Days of Wonder, $50, 2–5 players
Experience: Players plan routes and collect sets of cards to connect cities with their own train lines.
Demographic: All
Complexity: Low
Minimum Length: 60 minutes
Interaction: Low
Skills: Planning

Acquire, board game, Hasbro, $30, 3–6 players
Experience: Players invest in different companies that grow through tile play and merge.
Demographic: Teens, adults, seniors
Complexity: Low to medium
Minimum Length: 60 minutes
Interaction: Tile play, battling for majority control
Skills: Mathematics, planning, risk versus reward calculation

Carcassonne: The Discovery, board game, Rio Grande Games, $24.95
Experience: Players lay tiles to build roads and cities and claim control with clever piece play.
Demographic: Teens, adults, seniors
Complexity: Medium
Minimum Length: 45 minutes
Interaction: Low, piece-driven through competition for cities and roads
Skills: Planning, visualization

Quirkle, board game, MindWare, $24.95, 2–4 players

Experience: Players play tiles with colors and shapes in criss-cross patterns.
Demographic: All
Complexity: Low
Minimum Length: 60 minutes (although a shorter game could be played with fewer tiles)
Interaction: Players build off of each other's plays.
Skills: Planning, pattern recognition

Incan Gold, board game, FRED Distribution, $24.95, 3–8 players
Experience: Players decide between taking a sure thing or risk losing it all for more in simultaneous decisions.
Demographic: All
Complexity: Low
Minimum Length: 20 minutes
Interaction: Simultaneous selection of actions
Skills: Basic mathematics, probability, risk versus reward calculation

Ubongo, board game, Z-man Games, $44.99, 2–4 players
Experience: Players race to simultaneously solve puzzles under time pressure.
Demographic: Children (older), teens, adults
Complexity: Low
Minimum Length: 15 minutes
Interaction: Very little, as it's mainly a solo puzzle-solving game
Skills: Creative thinking, puzzle-solving, visualization

War Games

Another type of strategy gaming experience is a war game, also known as a *conflict simulation*. War games focus on a battle between two or more forces, usually in a specific historical, fantasy, or science fiction setting. These conflicts can be at the level of individual units on a single area of a battlefield, squads of units on a battlefield, armies in a larger theater of war, or battalions swooping across the galaxy. Some war games are played until one side is wiped out or gives up, and others are played until specified objectives are reached. Games can be symmetric, where both sides start out with the same strength of troops, or asymmetric, where the troops are of different strengths and the goals provide the game balance. Many games are placed in specific battles or campaigns and have rules to simulate the situation in the battle; in these games, the game is not balanced, and one player is attempting to see if he can rewrite history under challenging conditions. War games vary widely in the degree of realism represented, so that two games on the same topic can greatly range in complexity with the inclusion of historical elements in the ruleset. War games that are heavily steeped in the narrative of their setting are presented in the narrative gaming experiences chapter; the war games presented here are more focused on mechanics, strategy, and tactics.

After World War II, toys related to the military were seen as inappropriate in Germany. Game development during this time focusing on other forms of conflict resolution became popular, which planted the seeds for the resource management games of today. While these family strategy board games were advancing in Germany, American game developers were exploring different types of war games. The U.S. has been the leader in war game design for decades, but in recent years, designers from other countries have been creating interesting conflict simulations as they have discovered American war games.

Some players are dedicated to war games, while others focus on games set in a specific historical time, since they may have a thorough understanding of what was going on in that time period. Bringing these people into the library can have several benefits: Not only can they help teach and run conflict simulation games, but they also can give presentations and advise the librarian on related books and videos that would be a good match for certain types of games.

Librarians can search their local communities for war game clubs or conflict simulation clubs to locate these individuals.

Some mass-market war games serve as an introduction to the hobby. The game Risk is the first war game that many have experienced (and the game that turned many off to the concept of war games); there is a new, much shorter objective-based version of Risk that would be more appropriate for a library gaming function. The other mass-market war game that many have played is Axis and Allies. This is set in World War II, and each player represents a country, with all its strengths and weaknesses. The model of these games is that players can move all of their troops on the map on their turn, so turns can take a long time as a player plans out moving each unit in the army.

Another model of the war game is the card-driven war game. In these games, players draw a hand of cards, and the cards dictate what troops can be moved on the map. Rather than move the entire force every turn, players move a few units on each turn. This speeds up the pace of the game considerably and adds a new level of strategic planning as players can see what other cards are in their hand for future turns and plan accordingly. In some of these games, the cards introduce significant historical elements to the game and provide players with choices on how to use the card. An accessible game to use in starting to explore card-driven war games is Memoir '44, which is a two-player game set in World War II.

Some war games also use miniatures to represent the troops. These can have a large-scale map with markings to guide movement, or they can be more open with players using rulers to measure how far to move. One mass-market miniatures game is Heroscape, which is one of the few games that spans many different genres. In Heroscape, players first build the terrain with heavy-duty plastic terrain tiles. Players then select a team of heroes or monsters and take turns moving some of their units each turn and fighting or shooting as they get into range (Figure 5.1).

Figure 5.1 Heroscape (Reprinted with permission of Wizards of the Coast)

One popular miniatures game for an older crowd is Warhammer 40K. Produced by Games Workshop, this game is much more complex and expensive than Heroscape; however, there are many Games Workshop stores around the country. Libraries interested in Warhammer 40K can start by contacting one of these shops to see if someone is willing to come to the library and set up a demonstration and teaching session. A recent advance in miniatures games is Battleground: Fantasy Warfare, where the miniatures have been photographed and individuals play with cards rather than actual miniatures (Figure 5.2).

The advantage of this system is that the cost is low: For about $30, the library can purchase two armies and everything needed to play the game. In addition, it takes up little storage space, as each army is represented by a deck of cards.

This description of war games just scrapes the surface of a well-researched and deep hobby that includes a wide variety of game types and historical settings. Many of these games are either complex or start simple and become complex during play; that complexity brings a richness that isn't found in many other types of games. Because of this, these games tie in very well to more traditional

Figure 5.2 Battleground: Fantasy Warfare (Reprinted with permission of Chad Ellis)

library resources; once someone plays a game set in a specific historical setting, it makes them more likely to want to learn more about that setting. The best online resource for war games is ConsimWorld (www.consimworld.com). Libraries could use their club directory to locate some local experts on war games to aid in starting a program.

Risk (2008 Edition), board game, Parker Brothers, $29.99, 3–5 players
Experience: Players battle over countries and continents in an attempt to meet objectives.
Demographic: Teens, adults, select seniors

Complexity: Low to medium
Minimum Length: 90 minutes
Interaction: Direct conflict between troops on the board, negotiation
Skills: Tactical and strategic planning, negotiation

Memoir 44, board game, Days of Wonder, $50, 2 players
Experience: Players engage in head-to-head combat by playing cards to move troops and attack.
Demographic: Teens, adults, select seniors
Complexity: Low to medium
Minimum Length: 60 minutes
Interaction: Direct conflict
Skills: Tactical and strategic planning

Heroscape, miniatures game, Hasbro, $39.95, 2+ players
Experience: Players assemble a 3D world and battle for control with a group of detailed miniatures.
Demographic: Children (older), teens, adults, select seniors, intergenerational
Complexity: Low to medium
Minimum Length: 30 minutes
Interaction: Direct conflict
Skills: Tactical and strategic planning, creativity

Battleground: Fantasy Warfare, card game, Your Move Games, $14.95 per army (2 needed), 2 players
Experience: Players fight using cards representing miniatures by moving and attacking around a battlefield.
Demographic: Teens, adults, select seniors
Complexity: Medium
Minimum Length: 60 minutes
Interaction: Direct conflict
Skills: Tactical and strategic planning

Card Games

Card games have long been a popular pastime in the U.S. Public domain strategy card games like Bridge, Hearts, Spades, Euchre, Cribbage, and Rummy continue to be popular choices for families and friends. Poker is an interesting mix of a strategy and social gaming experiences; on the surface, it appears to be a strategic game, but the reality is that the underlying social aspect of Poker is much more important to winning the game.

Mah Jongg tiles are functionally the same as a deck of cards, and in some parts of the country, this is an extremely popular strategy game. (As an aside, the typical game played with Mah Jongg tiles is not the popular pair-matching computer game; Mah Jongg is a rummy-style gambling game.) As with Chess, there are national clubs for games such as Bridge and Mah Jongg that can provide a supply of passionate members, and many libraries already host these clubs.

Just as there are modern abstract games, there are also modern card games. Each year, many new card games are created, but only a few become popular enough to justify continued printings. Some, such as Pit, Mille Bornes, and Uno, are well-known mass-market modern card games. Other modern card games with humorous themes like Munchkin, Fluxx, and Killer Bunnies and The Quest for the Magic Carrot have not yet gained the same level of acceptance, but interest in these games among children and teens is growing quickly, and the games continue to be printed as they sell out. These humorous games are not very strategic but create silly situations to engage the players.

Some card games designed for adults embody many of the mechanics found in family strategy games. These include the trading game Bohnanza, the cooperative game Saboteur, the role-taking game Citadels, and the partnership card game Tichu, where teams work together to discard all of their cards. The 2009 game of the year from Germany was a card game called Dominion, where players take turns building up a deck of cards and use that deck to get the most points during game play.

A very different low-cost card game is called 1000 Blank White Cards. Several websites refer to this public-domain game (1kbwc.gemini6ice.com), which begins with a large stack of blank cards (or any other 3x5, mostly blank, uniform cards that a library might happen to have thousands of). Each player starts with 15 cards and a few markers. Players give each card a name, draw a picture, and give the card an effect, such as "+200 Points," "Cancel someone else's card," or "Choose someone who must sing a song to the group." The cards are shuffled and another five blank cards per player are added into the deck. On each turn, a player plays a card, and then draws their hand back up to five cards. If a player gets a blank card, that person can create whatever card is needed at the time. (It is useful to set a limit on the number of points one card can give or take away.) Play until someone can't draw up their hand, and then stop and add up points to determine the winner! For the next session, each player makes up five new cards and adds 15 older randomly selected cards from the deck. This deck can continue to grow for future rounds but will need to be weeded occasionally.

Many of these card games can offer as much interest as board games, but they have several advantages. They are much smaller, therefore easier to store, and they are much less expensive. Libraries interested in exploring recent developments in game design can start with these modern card games to see how well they work with patrons.

Fluxx, card game , Looney Labs, $16, 2–6 players

Experience: Cards played not only help players but change the rules and set the goal in this chaotic game.

Demographic: Children (*Family Fluxx* version), teens
Complexity: Low, but can change as the game goes on
Minimum Length: 15 minutes
Interaction: Inspires social interaction due to the chaos
Skills: Coping with change

Bohnanza, card game, Rio Grande Games, $19.95, 2–7 players
Experience: Players trade to collect the same types of beans to plant in their fields and decide when to cash in.
Demographic: Teens, adults, seniors
Complexity: Low to medium
Minimum Length: 45 minutes
Interaction: Trading is the key element of the game.
Skills: Negotiation, planning, risk versus reward calculation

Saboteur, card game, Z-man Games, $14.99, 3–10 players
Experience: Mostly cooperative game with a few hidden saboteurs working against the group
Demographic: Teens, adults, seniors
Complexity: Low to medium
Minimum Length: 20 minutes per round
Interaction: Considerable social interaction is involved as players try to determine the hidden saboteurs.
Skills: Planning, bluffing, deduction, reading others

Citadels, card game, Fantasy Flight Games, $19.99, 2–7 players
Experience: Players secretly select roles, construct buildings, and attempt to spoil each other's plans.
Demographic: Teens, adults
Complexity: Medium
Minimum Length: 30 minutes
Interaction: Direct conflict, social bluffing
Skills: Risk versus reward calculation through role selection, reading others

Collectible Card Games

Collectible card games (CCGs) are popular strategy gaming experiences with children and teens. These games mix the collectibility of baseball cards with the fun of a strategy game. Most of these games are designed for two players and pit them in a head-to-head combat. The genre began with Magic: The Gathering, where the cards represent spells and monsters that can be summoned to defeat an opposing wizard. Pokémon and YuGiOh! are popular games with younger players who call forth creatures to battle. The popular World of Warcraft trading card game appeals to older players and those who have spent considerable time with the World of Warcraft computer game and can be used as a draw to bring in players for a face-to-face activity related to their favorite online game. One social element of these games is the trading element: Because most players have their own cards and are looking for opportunities to trade with other players, the library can host a CCG Trading Day where players can bring their cards to trade and play with others.

Wizards of the Coast, the company that makes Magic: The Gathering, is very supportive of libraries. It has created the Wizards Play Network as a way for players to locate other players and places to play Magic. Libraries can join at several different levels of involvement based upon how many events they want to run each year. Joining the Wizards Play Network allows libraries to get free games and prize support for tournaments. Libraries can sign up to be a part of this network (www.wizards.com/default.asp?x=dci/wpn/main).

The main challenge of CCGs is cost. Starter packs for most CCGs will allow two players to explore the basics of the game. Once players are lured into the game, though, the costs for CCGs can be quite high. It is not feasible for most libraries to purchase too many of these cards so running programs where people bring their own cards to trade and play is a more economical approach.

Digital Games

Traditionally, most digital strategy games have been developed for a single player and are therefore not a focus of this book. As networking has become easier, though, multiplayer digital strategy games have grown in popularity. A few digital strategy games are designed for people sharing a console or screen; however, most multiplayer games are designed around players having their own systems. This allows for the *fog-of-war* aspect, in which each player knows about only a few areas of the battlefield.

Militaristic Digital Strategy Games

The basic concept behind many militaristic strategy games is that players control a base of operations and expand from that base to collect resources, build additional buildings, build armies, and then use those armies to conquer other players' base of operations. Some of these games require players to react in real time, such as the popular StarCraft, Warcraft III, or Age of Empires III. Other strategy games don't have the real-time element and are known as turn-based games, where players take turns making decisions. The Civilization series is the most popular example of this type of game and has versions on most gaming platforms. Real-time strategy games tend to consist of shorter missions or skirmishes, while turn-based games are longer games requiring many hours to complete. Libraries need to consider the length of a single game or determine ways to limit the experience when designing a program around these strategy games.

Another type of strategy game growing in popularity is tower defense. In these games, players defend a base on the screen by building defenses with a limited number of resources. After the player has had some time to build, a wave of enemies attacks and the strength of the player's defenses is tested. Between rounds, players have a few moments to improve the defenses before a new wave. While the popularity of tower defense games grew through custom-made maps for StarCraft and Warcraft III, Desktop Tower Defense, which is a web-based game designed in Adobe Flash, was the game that brought this genre to the attention of many. Plants vs. Zombies is a popular single-player version of a tower defense game that is easier for casual players than many of the other more complex games. PixelJunk Monsters, a downloadable PlayStation 3 title, is one of the few multiplayer tower defense games where players work together on the same screen; this model of a cooperative multiplayer game is ideal for many library programs.

Civilization Revolution, various consoles, 2K Games, $29.99, 1–4 players
Experience: Players build up an infrastructure and forces, and can win through military, economic, cultural, or scientific means.
Demographic: Teens, adults
Complexity: Medium
Minimum Length: Multiple hours for a full game so limits should be used.
Interaction: Direct conflict and limited space resources
Skills: Strategic and tactical planning, historical and geographical exploration, resource management

PixelJunk Monsters, PlayStation 3 downloadable game, Q-Games, $10, 1–2 players
Experience: Players build up and upgrade defenses against wave after wave of attackers.
Demographic: Children, teens, adults
Complexity: Low to medium
Minimum Length: 3–5 minutes per round, but the game has round after round
Interaction: Teamwork
Skills: Strategic and tactical planning, resource management

Simulations

Simulation games are another popular type of digital strategy game. SimCity is a classic example in which players plan out a city and the computer simulates how its inhabitants react to changes. The popularity of this game has triggered many more simulation games. Over the years, players have been able to build a high-rise tower, rule the Earth, or even run an ant farm! The current popular iteration in the series is The Sims, which allows players to focus on specific people and their house in a city. Some would question if these are actually games or if they are toys; the existence of in-game goals pushes these into the game category.

Another simulation is Second Life, where players can build virtual spaces and explore a large world—which, just like the real world, has a considerable amount of adult-themed content. Second Life on its own is not a game, but it is very easy to create games within this virtual world by adding structure and a goal. Teen Second Life is a space designed for teens, and the only adults allowed in are those who are vetted and have a need to work with teens in this space. These simulation tools can work well in a creative program where patrons create and share spaces. Putting several players around a computer and asking them to cooperate can add a team element and increase interaction. These simulations can also be playgrounds for exploring topics presented during a talk on architecture, urban planning, or fashion design.

Digital Versions of Strategy Board Games

Digital versions of traditional board games, such as Chess, have been a mainstay on most digital platforms. Some strategy board games have been adapted to electronic forms that allow people to play against others from their homes, such as Ticket to Ride or The Settlers of Catan, both of which are available via Xbox Live. Many war games have found an electronic home, as it is easier to have the computer track hundreds of cardboard chits than to move them physically on a map.

Some online strategy games also feel like board games. One of the earliest of these was a game about colonizing a planet, M.U.L.E., which was recently reborn as the board game Planet Steam. Age of Booty, a pirate-themed, fast-paced strategic game of nautical plunder, is available on several platforms and provides a board-game-like live-time strategic gaming experience for multiple players at the same system in a short period of time. The popular Pokémon card game has an even more popular Pokémon digital game equivalent; another low-cost library gaming program idea is to host a Pokémon tournament where players bring their own Nintendo systems and Pokémon collection to battle.

Age of Booty, online game (consoles and PC), Capcom, $10, 4 local players
Experience: Pirates sail to islands, conquering them for resource production to upgrade their ship and defenses and other pirates and their islands in order to hold the most islands simultaneously.
Demographic: Teens, adults
Complexity: Low to medium
Minimum Length: 10 minutes
Interaction: Direct and indirect conflict in-game
Skills: Resource awareness and management, tactical decisions, monitoring multiple input streams

Pokémon, electronic versions, Nintendo DS and Nintendo Wii, price varies,1 player or multiplayer
Experience: In the single-player game, players explore the world and develop and train a set of Pokémon (Pocket Monsters). Players can bring their DS devices together to

trade and battle Pokémon or can interact via the Wii Pokémon game.

Demographic: Children, teens (younger)
Complexity: Medium
Minimum Length: Varies
Interaction: Social interaction for trading
Skills: Planning, strategic and tactical decision making

Puzzle Games

Puzzle games, one of the more popular genres of online games, can provide a strategy game experience. These single-player casual games, such as Peggle or Bejeweled, are designed for someone to be able to start and complete one level of the game in a short period of time. These short rounds mean that a single-player game can be used in a tournament setting to allow many people to interact through a single-player gaming experience. Some console-based multiplayer puzzle games such as Tetris Party and Puzzle Fighter allow players to face off using their puzzle-solving skills, while the Worms series of games lets players select an angle and a shot strength to attempt to blow up their opponents on the other side of the screen.

Many of these games have a live-time element to make decision making more difficult. Yahoo!'s Puzzle Pirates is a combination of casual puzzle games and a massive multiplayer game. Players staff the different stations of a boat and solve puzzles effectively to do their task, and the combined efforts of the team dictate the success of the mission. These casual games attract players who don't typically consider themselves to be gamers and draw an adult audience, with largest demographic of casual games being women aged 30 to 45.[3]

Peggle, many digital platforms, Popcap games, price varies, 1 player
Experience: Players drop a ball in order to knock pegs off of a board.
Demographic: All
Complexity: Low
Minimum Length: 2 minutes per round
Interaction: None, although it can be used in a tournament setting for best score
Skills: Visualization of physics, timing

Worms, various versions, many digital platforms, Team 17, price varies, multiple players
Experience: Players take turns setting the angle and strength of shots to destroy the other team.
Demographic: All
Complexity: Low to medium
Minimum Length: 15 minutes per round
Interaction: Teamwork
Skills: Visualization of angles, planning

Many other types of digital games require strategy, such as fighting games, first-person shooting games, and sports games that emphasize the action part of the game. In these games, if players don't have the skills to react in real time, then their strategic planning doesn't matter; the strategy is important once the action components of the games are mastered. These types of games will be discussed in the next chapter.

Demographics

Children

A few companies make excellent strategy games for children. Haba and Selecta are both German companies that produce wonderful wooden games for younger age ranges. Some of these are as much fun for adults as they are for children, such as Tier auf Tier and Der Schwarze Pirat. Many of these games teach basic elements of strategy and are better choices than the popular Candy Land for providing a good gaming experience. Public domain games such as Checkers, Backgammon, and Chess are good choices for children as they get older. Many of the strategy games designed for older players are also accessible to children, especially if these young players have someone to help them learn the game. While younger players may struggle at first, strategy games are still excellent teaching tools. Collectible card games and digital versions of games like Pokémon can be a great draw for children who play the game at home.

Teens

By the time players become teenagers, most of them know if they are interested in strategy games. Some players will love them, and others will stay away from them. If a library holds a strategy gaming experience for teenagers, it is important to recognize that this will only draw a specific type of player. Libraries holding a Magic: The Gathering tournament or a teen Chess tournament will draw those teens who are into that type of gaming. Libraries that want to attract a wider spectrum of teens should combine a strategy gaming experience with another type of gaming experience.

Adults

Some adults are heavily engaged with strategy games. Members of a Chess club, for example, may be willing to help the library run a Chess event for others. Adult Scrabble, Mah Jongg, or Bridge players will gladly visit the library to attend a tournament and play their favorite games. Lighter strategy board games such as Blokus and Ticket to Ride work well with many adult populations, especially when marketed with images of popular casual online games with similar gameplay. A puzzle game tournament can draw closet Peggle fans out to the library. A weekly strategy board game group for adults can draw a variety of players from different economic and demographic groups from the local community.

Seniors

The same lighter strategy game that works for many adults can also be successful with seniors looking to keep their minds active. Games like Quirkle or Blokus are attractive and easy to learn and can work quite well. Another program idea is to ask seniors about their favorite games and put together a gaming program based upon those games. Many members of this group played games such as Dominoes, Pitch, Canasta, or Euchre growing up and would enjoy the chance to play again. The popularity of these games is regional so communicating with seniors about their favorite games is important and also helps engage them in the program when it runs.

Intergenerational

Because different age groups react to strategy games in different ways and play at different skill levels, it can be difficult to put together an intergenerational strategy gaming experience. The exception would be a regionally popular card game or a light strategy board or card game. With careful game selection, an intergenerational program could succeed. One type of intergenerational program that can work is to have families attend together and try out different types of light strategy games. This model is what the Essen Game Fair in Germany and the CHITAG event in Chicago use: Families attend these events together to look at a variety of games and determine what games to bring home and add to their collections. Families could be greeted with a menu of offerings served up by a library staff member and use the event to explore new games and to bond as a family.

Library Goals

Strategy gaming experiences teach many different life skills. Schools have used Chess for years as a way of teaching planning and strategic thinking. Resource management, short-term and long-term planning, negotiation, and making wise investments are skills that players develop as they simulate various situations and test different strategies to negotiate those situations. One valuable life skill that is embedded in most of these games is an understanding of probability and how it affects decisions. If the goal of the library program is to expand these types of life literacies, then a strategy gaming experience can work well.

Many of the strategy game titles mentioned in this chapter have enthusiastic players who would gladly travel to meet others who play the same game. Assuming that the game has some sort of a social element or that the game is placed into a larger structure, such as a tournament that encourages interaction, then these games can be useful in bringing in new patrons to libraries. When libraries show interest in things that are important to patrons, patrons are more likely to take a closer look at other library offerings.

As most of these games are set within a game world, interaction with the game can raise the interest of players to learn more about that specific world. Along these lines, these games can be used alongside more traditional library programs as a way for patrons to explore a topic more in-depth. Good marketing of related library materials will encourage these connections between games and books, videos, and other resources on the topic.

Endnotes

1. Mechanics' Institute Library & Chess Room, "About Us," www.milibrary.org/aboutchess.html (accessed March 29, 2010).
2. Harold James Ruthven Murray, *A History of Board-Games Other than Chess* (New York: Hacker Art Books, 1978).

3. International Game Developers Association, "2008–2009 Casual Games White Paper," archives.igda.org/casual/IGDA_Casual_Games_White_Paper_2008.pdf (accessed March 29, 2010).

Action Gaming Experiences

Action gaming experiences focus on the ability of players to manipulate the game state. These gaming experiences stress the physical skills of the players, such as hand–eye coordination and reflexes. There are some elements of strategic decision making involved in action games, but players must move controllers, push buttons, slide pucks, or do other activities to carry out these strategic choices. Many digital games fall into this category, while many fewer analog games fit here. Action games for teens, such as Dance Dance Revolution and various Wii games, are what many people think about when the modern concept of "gaming in the library" is mentioned.

Environment

Action games are noisy. Aside from the sound of a digital system, the excitement generated by players madly pressing buttons and getting into the game is difficult to control, so libraries that require a quiet gaming experience should not select an action game. The noise level of these games, though, raises the energy that goes along with them, and an action gaming experience generally provides an eye-catching, silence-breaking, attention-grabbing, energetic environment.

Both computer and console platforms can be used for action games. Many console action games allow multiple people to play using the same screen. Some of these use a split-screen concept, where each player in the game uses a small portion of the screen. In typical home play, this split-screen action can create a space that is too small for detailed play. If a library has a projector available for these games, the split-screen play can work much better, as players can easily see their section of the screen. In addition, it is much easier for spectators to gather around and watch the game.

Computer action games almost always require a separate computer for each player, and it is more difficult for spectators to get a good idea of what is going on in a networked computer game; they can look over someone's shoulder to see one point of view but won't get a good grasp of the entire field of play. The play experience for individuals can be much more immersive if they have their own screen and headphones. Therefore, libraries must decide what is more important for the experience: an immersive activity for individuals or a more social-interactive display where spectators can enjoy the game.

Many solo action games are available, but these are not the focus of this book since the goal here is to look at multiplayer gaming experiences. As most libraries can't afford the space or equipment to purchase consoles for individual players, the focus is primarily on games that have multiplayer, shared-screen modes. Libraries could base a tournament around a solo action game where each player takes a turn and scores are recorded, although this lacks some of the interaction in a multiplayer game. To use an analogy, this is like the difference between golf, where each player is measured on a solo experience based upon how well they perform, and team sports, where the interaction between players is part of the game.

Action games can work well as team activities in a number of ways. Some games allow players to work together on a team. Other games can be adapted to team play, where each member of the team is in control for part of the game. Another route is to have players sign up as teams, but members of the team play in heats against members of other teams. Because many action games can be played in shorter rounds, this allows for a very flexible gaming experience that can be used to meet a variety of needs.

Libraries looking for an exciting tournament should consider an action gaming experience as their first choice. Because of the energy and fast pace of these games, they work well in a tournament structure. Tournaments can draw in a wider variety of passionate gamers than an open-play event. The best book about video game tournaments in the library is Eli Neiburger's *Gamers ... in the Library?!* (2009, ALA Editions). Neiburger goes through everything librarians need to know about running a tournament, then reviews a number of games for libraries to consider.

Digital Games

Most action gaming experiences come through digital games. Through surveys done over the last few years, I've learned which types of games are most popular in libraries, and the game types presented here have come from those surveys. Rhythm games and Wii Sports are currently the two most popular digital games used in libraries.

Rhythm Games

One of the first modern action games to become popular in libraries was Dance Dance Revolution (DDR). In fact, it was a DDR game set up by Jenny Levine at the American Library Association (ALA) TechSource booth at an ALA midwinter conference that first drew my attention and inspired my exploration of games in libraries. DDR is one in a category of rhythm games where players take an action to the beat of music. This action might be stepping on one specific dance pad, holding down a selected button on the fret of a guitar while strumming, hitting a certain drum pad, or singing a note; the more accurate players are with the timing of the action, the higher their score. For example, when a player takes this action in some games, the next note in the song is played, so that a player can judge their success by how good the song actually sounds.

The two current popular franchises for rhythm games are Rock Band and Guitar Hero. Guitar Hero started as a game where players played the guitar, while Rock Band was the first game to allow a four-member band to play, with one vocalist, a lead guitar, a bass guitar, and drums. The teamwork element in Rock Band was so popular that future versions of Guitar Hero added drums and vocals, so now both games provide very similar experiences. Libraries selecting between them can use either price or the available music list to influence their decision. An exciting development in this genre is the Beatles Rock Band game. Because the music of the Beatles crosses many generational boundaries, this is a highly recommended version of the game for libraries wishing to create intergenerational gaming programs.

Dance Dance Revolution, console game, Konami, price varies, 1–2 players (1–4 on Wii)

Experience: Players step on pads to the beat of a song. Expensive metal dance pads (about $200 each) can be purchased and are heavy and more durable.

Demographic: Children, teens, adults

Complexity: Low

Minimum Length: 3–5 minutes per round
Interaction: None
Skills: Foot–eye coordination, planning ahead, sense of rhythm and tone

Guitar Hero, console game, Activision, price varies, 1–2 players (newer versions allow 1–4 players)
Experience: Players press buttons on a guitar fret matching colored dots coming on the screen, and strum a plastic bar on the beat of the song. Newer versions allow drums and vocals.
Demographic: Children, teens, adults
Complexity: Low
Minimum Length: 3–5 minutes per round
Interaction: Very little in traditional *Guitar Hero*. Newer versions allow a group to perform as a band and introduce more teamwork elements.
Skills: Hand–eye coordination, planning ahead, sense of rhythm

Rock Band, console game, Harmonix, price varies, 1–4 players
Experience: Players play guitar, bass, and drum representations and sing following on-screen guides, matching colors of buttons or pitch and rhythm.
Demographic: Children, teens, adults
Complexity: Low
Minimum Length: 3–5 minutes per round
Interaction: Teamwork elements
Skills: Hand–eye coordination, planning ahead, sense of rhythm and tone

Wii Games

Due to its ease of use, the Wii has become a popular platform for digital gaming experiences in libraries, and the game that comes with each Wii is Wii Sports. The Wii uses motion-based controls as players wave Wiimotes through the air to control their on-screen character. This integration of the motion-control scheme used in most games sets the Wii apart from the other consoles of the same generation, the Xbox 360 and the PlayStation 3 (PS3). (The PS3's controllers are motion-sensing as well, but few games take advantage of this ability.)

This motion-sensing control has a significant impact on two aspects of the gaming experience. First, it makes it easier for many people to play the game, as broad motions can be used instead of twitching fingers. Second, it levels the playing field. Because the controls are less precise, skilled gamers are not able to control their characters with the precision they are used to in other games. This ends up creating more of a social atmosphere, as everyone has a chance to win; however, this can frustrate hardcore gamers. Nintendo's answer to this was the Wii Motion Plus, a $20 add-on to the Wiimote that makes it more sensitive in selected games; however, it does not seem to be as popular as Nintendo might have hoped.

Every Wednesday, our library runs a Wii gaming program for all patrons in the library. It's interesting to see that, while primarily made up of teens, the program also draws a significant number of tween and adult patrons as well. We almost always play Super Smash Bros. Brawl and run the gaming program as a tournament; the players who die first in the game have to give up their controller to the next person waiting to play. Although it's a competition, the program has provided a forum where many friendships have developed and grown among our patrons.

Ryan Donovan,
Mott Haven Branch, The New York Public Library

When using the popular Wii Sports, just as with any game, it is important to understand the role of each specific sport activity and how long the activity will last. Tennis, for example, is one of the best tools for getting new Wii players used to the Wiimote. Bowling is a good game for intergenerational use as it was an important activity to many seniors in their youth; they can recreate this sport without the same stresses on their bodies. Golf, while a popular choice, can take a very long time to play through the entire course; if there are others waiting, one suggestion is to limit the number of holes that make up a game. Boxing is a very tiring activity but is quite fun for spectators to watch.

Because of the casual nature of using the motion control, many lighter games have been created for the Wii. These party games are made up of many smaller mini-games wrapped into a larger theme. Carnival Games, for example, replicates many of the types of games one might play on the midway of the local fair. Rayman Raving Rabbids is a chaotic game with very unusual mini-games like plunger-shooting and warthog racing. The WarioWare franchise focuses on microgames, where players have a few seconds to ascertain what to do and accomplish it before a timer runs out. Mario Party takes a board game theme and has players competing in different mini-games as they travel around a board. The idea behind Big Brain Academy is that it helps players in their thinking skills through more intellectual mini-games; however, the structure of the activities makes this a difficult game to use successfully in a library gaming program. One of the more varied games along these lines is Boom Blox, where players can play cooperatively or competitively, sometimes building and sometimes destroying blocks to achieve goals.

Wii Sports, Wii game, Nintendo, $49.99, 1–4 players (*Author's Note*: The game comes with one $20 accessory; players need one of these for each Wiimote to play, so add $60 to the cost for four players.)

Experience: Players simulate a number of sports, including new versions of golf and bowling, using an add-on to the original Wiimote controller to make it more sensitive.

Demographic: All, intergenerational

Complexity: Low

Minimum Length: Varies by sport

Interaction: Varies by sport. Fencing is very interactive through direct competition, while bowling and golf are not.

Skills: Hand–eye coordination

Carnival Games, Wii game, Nintendo, Take 2 Entertainment, $29.99, 1–4 players

Experience: Players recreate carnival games through waving the Wiimotes.

Demographic: All

Complexity: Low

Minimum Length: 3–5 minutes

Interaction: None. Games are about players playing on their own while others wait.

Skills: Hand–eye coordination

Boom Blox, Wii game, Nintendo, Electronic Arts, $29.99, 1–4 players

Experience: Players destroy towers of blocks, hit targets, and yank blocks.

Demographic: All

Complexity: Low to medium

Minimum Length: 10 minutes

Interaction: Some games have direct conflict as players attack each other; other games have players working together.

Skills: Hand–eye coordination, planning, puzzle solving

Mario Party 8, Wii game, Nintendo, $49.99
Experience: Players roll and move on a simplistic board game that has players compete or cooperate each round in mini-games.
Demographic: All
Complexity: Low to medium
Minimum Length: 30 minutes
Interaction: Changes throughout the game. Some mini-games are completely competitive, while others divide the players into teams.
Skills: Hand–eye coordination, planning, and a variety of other skills based upon the randomly selected mini-games

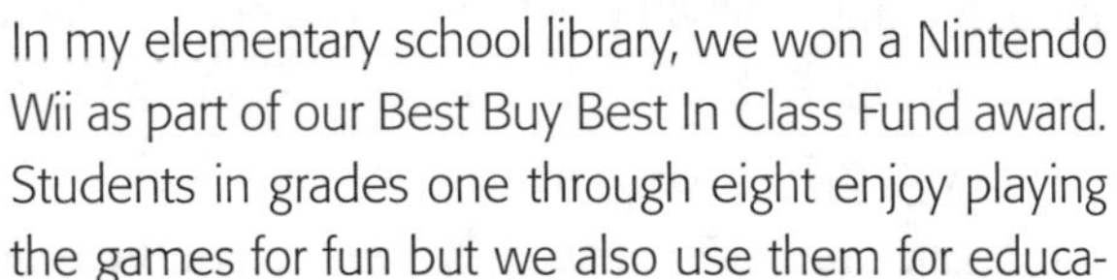

In my elementary school library, we won a Nintendo Wii as part of our Best Buy Best In Class Fund award. Students in grades one through eight enjoy playing the games for fun but we also use them for educational purposes. Grade six students examined the coaches on Wii Fit for media portrayals of athletes. Grade five music students used Wii Music to create their own compositions. Primary students played Wii Sports as part of their DPA [daily physical activity] and as a way to practice taking turns and being good sports. The students themselves have noted other academic uses for it—while playing Wii Sports, one student noted that she needed to know how to read fractions to see how well the players were doing on Wii Boxing. The kids are engaged and excited about learning/playing.

Diana Maliszewski,
Agnes Macphail Public School

Sports Games

Other types of action games will attract a more hardcore group of gamers. Sports games, such as the Madden franchise, will draw both fans of that sport and fans of the game. Libraries could theme an entire fall event around a Madden Football tournament, with speakers and readings about football, Fantasy Football leagues, suggestions of football-related books and movies, and games featuring football.

Libraries have a challenging decision to make when purchasing a sports title. Most sports titles feature the team rosters and players who are actually in the league that year, and as the players change from year to year, the game franchise releases a new version of the game with updated teams but similar gameplay to last year's title. Because of this, many gamers will sell the used copy of their game to a local game store and purchase the new version. Game stores have an abundance of very inexpensive sports titles that are a few years old, and for a library on a tight gaming budget, these represent a fantastic value in providing an action gaming experience. If a library does not have the newest rosters available, hardcore gamers may be disappointed and see the library's selection as outdated and not of value to them. Therefore, libraries must balance between taking advantage of a great deal and having the newest team rosters; the decision needs to come down to the purpose of the gaming program and the target audience.

Another popular sport is racing, and there is less turnover in racing titles than in football or basketball. There are several types of racing games available, but as discussed earlier, the ones that best fit in a library program are those that allow four racers at a time to race in a split-screen mode, where each player has one-fourth of the screen. The most popular racing game of this type is Mario Kart. These go-cart racing games have been popular for years, and as they are set in Nintendo's Mario universe, the game can be played by all ages. Mario Kart for the Wii allows players to drive by holding the control horizontally and turning it like a wheel (or putting it into a plastic wheel and turning that). Another excellent choice is Mario

Kart DS, which allows each player to use a Nintendo DS system. Up to eight players can race using Wi-Fi.

Mario Kart tournaments can be great draws for both male and female players (unlike some of the other action game categories that draw primarily males), and they can cross different generations of players. More serious driving games that feature splitscreen multiplayer include Motorstorm Pacific Rift and Blur. Calling All Cars is a top-down, fast-paced cartoon driving game available for PS3, where players attempt to capture criminals and deliver them to jail.

Madden NFL, console game, Electronic Arts, price varies, 1–4 players
Experience: Players call and execute plays in a high-speed football simulation.
Demographic: Teens, adults
Complexity: Medium to high
Minimum Length: 30 minutes
Interaction: Direct conflict
Skills: Hand–eye coordination, strategic thinking, teamwork

Mario Kart, Wii/DS game, Nintendo, $39.99–$49.99, 1–4 players (Wii), 1–8 players (DS)
Experience: Fast-paced split-screen racing game as players jockey for position and attack each other with weaponry.
Demographic: Children, teens, adults
Complexity: Low
Minimum Length: 5 minutes
Interaction: Indirect conflict through racing with moments of direct conflict through weapons
Skills: Hand–eye coordination, planning

Calling All Cars, PlayStation 3 downloadable game, Sony Entertainment, $10, 1–4 players

Experience: Top-down light arcade-style racing shooter where players attempt to capture a criminal and bring them back to jail while other players try to get the criminal for themselves.
Demographic: Children, teens, adults
Complexity: Low
Minimum Length: 5 minutes
Interaction: Direct conflict
Skills: Hand–eye coordination

Motorstorm: Pacific Rift, PlayStation 3 game, Sony, $59.99, 1–4 players
Experience: Fast-paced racing with split-screen play that is more realistic than cart racers.
Demographic: Teens, adults
Complexity: Low to medium
Minimum Length: 5 minutes
Interaction: Indirect conflict through racing, bumping, ramming
Skills: Hand–eye coordination, planning

Fighting Games

Traditional fighting games reduce the focus of the game down to one-on-one combat in a fixed arena. While these games are violent, they vary in the amount of graphic violence depicted. On the Wii, Super Smash Bros. Brawl is an excellent choice for a family-style fighting game with no blood or gore. Players run around a stage on a series of different types of platforms, trying to damage each other and knock each other off of the platforms. Players can pick up special weapons and use features of the terrain wisely against opponents. The game easily handles four players gathered around a single screen with a "last man standing" play style. In addition, it allows players to connect over the internet for online contests. During National Gaming Day @ Your Library events in 2008 and 2009, Eli

Neiburger and the Ann Arbor District (MI) Library hosted an online library versus library Super Smash Bros. Brawl tournament.

For libraries without a Wii or that want a more traditional fighting game, Super Street Fighter II HD Turbo Remix, despite its absurd name, is a well-done remake of a series of games (based upon the extremely popular Street Fighter II, which was very popular in the early 1990s). Its cartoon style makes it more appropriate for use in a library tournament than games with more realistic graphic violence such as Mortal Kombat. Another advantage of this title is that it allows older and younger gamers to connect.

Super Smash Bros. Brawl, Wii game, Nintendo, $49.99, 1–4 players
Experience: Players compete to be king of the hill by knocking other players off platforms.
Demographic: Children, teens, select adults
Complexity: Low to medium
Minimum Length: 5 minutes
Interaction: Direct conflict
Skills: Hand–eye coordination, strategic thinking

Super Street Fighter II HD Turbo Remix, console game, downloadable, Capcom, $20, 1–2 players
Experience: Two players fight through attacking and blocking to knock each other out.
Demographic: Teens, adults
Complexity: Medium
Minimum Length: 5 minutes
Interaction: Direct conflict
Skills: Hand–eye coordination, rapid tactical thinking

First-Person Shooters and Other Real-Time Combat Games

In first-person shooter games, players see through the eyes of their avatars, much the same as looking through a camera held at eye level. While running around an environment, players shoot at other players and enemies. These immersive games may also have stealth or driving elements.

Due to the nature of first-person shooter games, most of them have considerable graphic violence and have received a Mature rating. At the time of this writing, all of the high-quality first-person shooter games for current consoles that allow multiple players to play on one console are rated Mature. Libraries that have a PlayStation 2 or an original Xbox can consider TimeSplitters 2. This is a good selection for this category, as it is rated for Teens and allows multiple players to play on the same console. One recent development in this arena is Water Warfare, a water-gun fight game for the Wii. While Water Warfare does allow two players to fight on a split screen, it has not received good reviews. I hope to see future developments of first-person shooter games that are not rated Mature.

Another route to providing a similar experience to first-person shooter games is through action role-playing games. These games put players in the shoes of a character running through a battlefield, having adventures, and becoming stronger over time. Some of these games are set in literary worlds that can then be used to connect the gaming program to other library resources. Lord of the Rings: Conquest, which is similar to other games in this series, is a Teen-rated game that handles four players at the same time as they either work together or work against each other, fighting across the battle-field. A cartoon-style downloadable game for the Xbox 360 is Castle Crashers, which is modeled after a style of game popular in the 1980s where most of the action takes place in two dimensions from left to right, but players have the ability to jump and move for-ward and back on the battlefield. It also handles four players on the screen at the same time and is a very easy game to learn. Because of its connection to games from the past, it would be a good intergenerational game choice for teens and adults.

Halo 3, Xbox 360 game, Microsoft, $59.99, 1–4 players
Experience: Players hunt each other through a first-person view in maze-like quarters with a variety of weaponry.
Demographic: Teens (although it is rated Mature), adults
Complexity: Medium
Minimum Length: 5 minutes
Interaction: Direct conflict. Some modes have teamwork.
Skills: Hand–eye coordination, tactical planning

Lord of the Rings: Conquest, console game, Electronic Arts, $29.99, 1–4 players
Experience: In a third-person view, players fend off the forces of evil through swordplay, arrows, and magic.
Demographic: Teens, adults
Complexity: Medium
Minimum Length: 10 minutes for one level
Interaction: Players must work together as a team to succeed.
Skills: Hand–eye coordination, strategic and tactical planning

Castle Crashers, Xbox 360 downloadable game, The Behemoth, $15, 1–4 players
Experience: Players work together to slay evil through button-mashing attacks and jumps in this cartoony side-scrolling combat game.
Demographic: Teens, adults
Complexity: Low to medium
Minimum Length: 10 minutes for one level
Interaction: There is a balance between competition and cooperation throughout the game.
Skills: Hand–eye coordination

Retro Games

Games from the 1970s and 1980s are known as *retro games* and have made a comeback in popularity. These games are ideal for use in creating an intergenerational action gaming experience as they connect teens to those who were teens when the retro games were first popular. Most of these retro games used to be in video arcades, and library users who have fond memories of spending their quarters playing Donkey Kong, Pac Man, or Joust will be drawn to these programs. Most early digital games fall into the action game category, so the popularity of retro game titles can draw in people who originally played the game and new players who are curious to see what the games were all about and to test their skills.

Retro games are available in many different ways. A number of companies have put out retro game packages for game consoles and computers; Namco Museum, for example, has 30 retro arcade game titles ranging from Galaga to Dig Dug to Ms. Pac-Man. Another route to retro games is through the online services for the consoles; the online storefronts for all three of the current consoles have many retro games available for purchase and download. A more direct route to older games is to dig out an old game system: Any system from the Atari 2600 up through the Nintendo GameCube can be hooked into projectors for a large-scale (but heavily pixelated) retro gaming experience that will draw the generations of players who used to enjoy those games.

There are several websites with nonlicensed versions of these games, such as 80s Arcade (www.free80sarcade.com), where programmers have created versions that can be played in a browser. The MAME emulator for computers allows users to take the content from a ROM chip in old arcade games and play that game via the emulator; however, it is technically illegal to use the ROMs for arcade games that one does not own. If a library staff member or volunteer suggests MAME for library use, be aware that the use of MAME being proposed is most likely illegal.

Another route to retro-style gaming is to use remakes or new games that take the style of retro games and add modern touches. A number of older games have been remade into newer versions for today's generation of consoles. Pac-Man Championship Edition and Galaga Legions are examples of titles that have taken old concepts and remade them. Namco Museum Remix for the Wii includes new versions of some games alongside their classic versions. Another route is to use new games made in the style of retro games, such as the aforementioned Castle Crashers. Another shooter choice with some great multiplayer options is Geometry Wars: Retro Evolved 2. This title has gameplay similar to the classic Asteroids with a simple control scheme—but with many modern twists. Retro gaming activities, whether authentic or modernized, are strong tools for a library seeking to bring players from different generations together through a digital action gaming experience.

Namco Museum series, console games, Namco, price varies, 1–2 players
Experience: Older arcade games and some remakes of older games; usually reaction-based games without much depth or story
Demographic: Children, teens, adults, select seniors
Complexity: Low
Minimum Length: 3 minutes
Interaction: Very little. Some games have some two-player direct conflict.
Skills: Hand–eye coordination

Geometry Wars: Retro Evolved 2, Xbox 360 downloadable game, Bizarre Creations, $10, 1–4 players

Experience: This retro-style, fast-paced overhead shooting game uses one joystick to move and one to shoot wave after wave of enemies.
Demographic: Teens, adults
Complexity: Low
Minimum Length: Depends upon the type of game. There is a 3-minute timed game.
Interaction: Little
Skills: Hand–eye coordination, rapid tactical planning

Analog Dexterity Games

Few analog games fall into the action game category, but one type—dexterity games—certainly does. Libraries seeking to provide a board-game alternative to people focused on video games can find quite a few dexterity games to serve this need. Some of the well-known dexterity games include Pick-Up Sticks and Jenga, neither of which involves much strategy. Some modern dexterity games, though, have significant strategic elements in addition to the physical manipulation element.

Villa Paletti, for example, looks like a building game with chunky columns holding up layers of floors that players build up, but there is considerable strategy lurking behind those primary colored blocks. Players must decide what columns to remove in order to force opponents to leave their columns behind to support the structure. In Hamster Rolle, players attempt to get rid of their pieces by playing them up the inside of a rolling wheel; the strategy comes in selecting pieces and placements that will cause trouble for others. Cornerstone is a game similar to a 3D Blokus, where players stack their pieces higher and higher with the goal of moving a playing piece higher onto the structure; as the game moves toward its conclusion, the dexterity elements come into play until one player knocks the tower down with a risky move.

Several games on the same theme combine strategy and dexterity, requiring players to flick a piece toward a target. Crokinole is a classic public-domain game that has a passing resemblance to Carrom (but is more like curling in its play); both of these are good games but require expensive and large wooden boards. Tumblin' Dice is similar in style, with players flicking dice toward the end of a board without going too far. The final score, though, is the number on the top of the die times the space where it sits; this element of luck allows less skilled gamers to play competitively with those who are practiced at the game. PitchCar has a large wooden racetrack, and players flick disks that represent racecars that zoom around the track. A very inexpensive game in the shuffleboard family is Sorry Sliders, which has pawns with large ball bearings that players roll down the board toward the center spots. While not as elegant or attractive as some of the other games listed here, it is a great starting point for a library wanting to add a dexterity game.

Another type of analog dexterity games includes those designed for children. Many of these games are just as entertaining for adults to play with their children or, once the children are in bed, to play with other adults. Haba, a German game company whose products can be found in many U.S. upscale toy stores, is one distributor of these types of games for older children that work well for adults. Tier auf Tier is a game involving stacking wooden animals, Dancing Eggs has players keep rubber eggs under their arms and chins while trying to catch additional bouncing eggs, Mouse Rally lets players flick wooden mice around a racetrack while avoiding holes and cats (controlled by players who have been knocked out), and Mouse in the House, which has been recently republished in the U.S. by Gamewright games as Hula Hippos, has players trying to flick their pieces to a position where a spinning ring will stop and fall on them. One of the most clever intergenerational dexterity games is Gulo Gulo, where players have to pick out colored eggs from a nest without setting off a trap; those older adults with big fumbly fingers will struggle against children with smaller fingers.

Villa Paletti, board game, University Games, $29.99, 2–4 players
Experience: Players remove colored columns that support a platform and move them to the top of the platform, building higher until the platform crashes.
Demographic: Children, teens, adults
Complexity: Low
Minimum Length: 30 minutes
Interaction: Indirect interaction as players leave other players' columns to support the base
Skills: Hand–eye coordination, strategic thinking

Cornerstone, board game, Good Company Games, $49.99, 2–4 players
Experience: Players build a multicolored tower with blocks and move their pawns higher and higher on the tower without crossing opponent's colors until the tower collapses.
Demographic: Teens, adults
Complexity: Low to medium
Minimum Length: 30 minutes
Interaction: Indirect conflict as players block other players with pieces and pawns
Skills: Strategy at first, then hand–eye coordination as the tower gets higher

Sorry Sliders, board game, Hasbro, $24.99, 2–4 players
Experience: Players slide pawns toward the middle, knocking other pawns out of the way.
Demographic: Children, teens, adults
Complexity: Low

Minimum Length: 15 minutes
Interaction: Direct conflict
Skills: Hand–eye coordination

Tumblin Dice, board game, Nash games/FRED distribution $64.99, 2–4 players
Experience: Players flick dice down a gentle wooden staircase and attempt to gain points by multiplying the number on the die by the level of the staircase it lands on.
Demographic: Children, teens, adults
Complexity: Low
Minimum Length: 10 minutes
Interaction: Direct conflict
Skills: Hand–eye coordination, simple multiplication

Tier auf Tier (aka *Animal Upon Animal*), board game, Haba, $22, 2–4 players
Experience: Players stack wooden animals in an attempt to get rid of all of their animals first.
Demographic: All
Complexity: Children, teens, adults, select seniors
Minimum Length: 10 minutes
Interaction: Creating situations for opponents to deal with
Skills: Hand–eye coordination, planning

Gulo Gulo, board game, Rio Grande Games, $39.95, 2–6 players
Experience: Players remove eggs from a bowl without knocking over a long stick to move on a modular track.
Demographic: Children, teens, adults, seniors, intergenerational (with children)
Complexity: Low
Minimum Length: 30 minutes
Interaction: Very little through the game
Skills: Hand–eye coordination, risk versus reward calculation

Big Games

The big game format lends itself well to action gaming experiences since the individuals are playing a life-sized game and are physically involved with the game state. Any big game could have physical game components; for example, players might have to hit a target with a beanbag, jump or crawl through obstacles, or quickly get from place to place. In fact, there is a very fine line between these types of experiences and playground sports. A game of Kickball, Four-square, Nerf Wars, or Dodgeball out in the library parking lot is certainly an action gaming experience that can be part of a program. If this is then tied into a larger program, it can provide for a nice break to interact with other participants in an unusual way. As with any library gaming experience, Dodgeball in the stacks needs to be tied into a larger program goal to be justifiable (although the idea of playing "hunt the librarian" with Nerf guns may be quite entertaining).

Another action game concept is playing Miniature Golf in the library. The folks at Library Mini Golf (www.libraryminigolf.org) will come to a library and run a Miniature Golf event through the stacks as a fundraiser. This activity can also act as a tour through the library, and by integrating the miniature golf into a puzzle hunt where players have to use the books around certain holes to answer questions, it combines an action gaming experience with an information literacy activity.

To draw more attention to a game, librarians can make a larger version of the game. On his Deep Fun site (www.deepfun.com/pickupsticks.html), Bernie DeKoven presents an idea for Giant Pick-Up Sticks using the cardboard tubes found in the middle of rolls of carpet. For libraries with a lot of space for an outdoor event, this could be an inexpensive, eye-catching program. The tubes are painted in several colors, and a few volunteers gather them up and hold hands around them. On a signal, the volunteers let go and run away, allowing the tubes to fall, and then the traditional rules of Pick-Up Sticks are used as teams have to pick up a stick without disturbing any of the others. Big versions of traditional games are ways to allow players to engage with the experience more fully than if they were sitting back, watching the game unfold on a tabletop.

Demographics

Children

Action gaming experiences are great for children as long as the games are simple enough for them to get engaged. As children get older, they will be drawn more toward digital action games. Many of the games by Haba and Selecta are centered on a basic action gaming experience, and a number of these are good choices for children to play with older participants. Many libraries have used action gaming experiences alongside storytime sessions as a way of getting children more involved with the story.

Teens

Many libraries currently match teens and action gaming experiences in their library gaming events, using popular video games as a way of bringing teens into the library. These gaming experiences are effective in drawing in a variety of teen players who enjoy testing their hand–eye coordination and dexterity. Teens who are into gaming can practice many of these games at home and then come to the library to compete in a tournament and demonstrate their prowess in front of their peers. Of the game types, action gaming experiences are the best archetype overall for the goal of drawing teen users to the library.

Adults

Younger adults are more likely to readily engage with action gaming experiences than older adults. Many of these people have grown up with video games and thus have well-honed hand–eye coordination. These groups are the ones most likely to respond well to a retro gaming experience. Many adults would like to try games like DDR but may need encouragement and coaching to give it a try, as they don't want to feel humiliated. Libraries may find greater success in getting adults to enjoy rhythm and music games in a gaming session just for adults. Adults respond well to analog action gaming experiences as these are on a smaller scale and are less likely to be embarrassing.

Seniors

Libraries need to carefully select action gaming experiences for seniors. Fast-paced games with significant real-time elements are typically not very successful with senior players. Wii Bowling is one of the most successful action games, as it allows seniors to take their time and to call upon skills that many developed at a younger age but can no longer easily do. Games like Tumblin' Dice work well for the same reason; players can take their time in setting up a shot, and the action of flicking a die is not strenuous.

Intergenerational

Because different generations approach action games in different ways, the games used for intergenerational action gaming experience need to be chosen with their target generations in mind. A game that will involve seniors should not have a significant live time element. As mentioned in the previous section, Wii Bowling has been one of the more successful choices. The Beatles Rock Band game is also an excellent intergenerational choice because of the selection of music. Many of the board games listed in this chapter that do not have a time element can work well; Gulo Gulo is an engaging game for children as they are naturally better at the game.

Library Goals

Of the different game archetypes, action gaming experiences are most difficult to tie into library goals. From a skill-building perspective, action gaming experiences develop hand–eye coordination, quick thinking, and dexterity. Many of these games also facilitate social interactions and allow for strategic exploration, but if these are the goals of the library, then games more focused on social interactions or strategic play should be selected.

If the goal of having games is to draw people to the library, action gaming experiences can work very well, especially for teen and younger adult audiences. Tournaments can draw hundreds of players who have played these games at home and want to test their skill against others in the community. These gaming experiences can also attract those who want to try games before purchasing them for their home. Libraries choosing these action gaming experiences need to be aware of the goals that these experiences meet so that they can justify the games to their stakeholders and critics. Action games are the most likely type to draw critical attention from the press and the community, so libraries selecting these games must be prepared to answer the question: "What does Rock Band have to do with the library?"

Narrative Gaming Experiences

Narrative gaming experiences focus on the interaction between the players and the world in which the game is set. Storytelling is an important aspect of these games; the game creator tells part of the story and sets the stage, and the players, through playing the game, tell the rest of the story. One way that I discuss gaming in the library context is that "this is storytime for the rest of us," and narrative gaming experiences are the best tools for a storytime-like experience. In addition, narrative gaming experiences are some of the best experiences for supporting traditional reading-based literacy goals through gaming.

Environment

Narrative gaming experiences have the potential to be loud. The game itself may not be as loud as an action-focused game, but as players interact in many of these games, the overall gaming experience can be louder than most strategy and knowledge gaming experiences. One example is that of role-playing games (RPGs), where one player talks to the group, and depending upon the game, the players may get into character, raising their voices and using silly accents. Librarians can try to keep the noise down, but once players get into character, it can be challenging to keep their enthusiasm from taking over.

One advantage to narrative games is that they don't require anything other than creativity. One great way for libraries to integrate a narrative gaming experience into a book club meeting would be to ask the group to continue the story where the book left off. The librarian can provide a new challenge, and the book club members can discuss ways that the characters might deal with that challenge. One route would be to split the book club into smaller groups, give each group the same plot challenges, and ask each to continue the story. After each group has had time to continue the story, have each group tell what their story was and see how they differ. Because the library is already full of easily explorable worlds and backstories, narrative gaming experiences naturally flow from traditional library resources.

Analog Role-Playing Games

RPGs best epitomize the narrative gaming experience. In a tabletop RPG, players create characters for use in the game world through a set of rules. After they have created their characters, one participant—the game master (GM)—sets the stage and presents the challenges while the players respond in the way that their characters would. For example, during a game set in the Wild West, the GM might say:

> Dust blows in the street of this old town. The air is thick with the smell of cattle, as a herd is being driven through the town just on the outskirts. You dismount from your

> horses and hear the plinking of an off-tune piano from the nearby saloon. Scanning the rest of the town, you see a group of men in long black coats enter the well-labeled bank. Shortly after, there are shots of gunfire from the bank. The cattle, hearing the noise, begin to panic and stampede in different directions. What do you do?

The rules for RPGs are usually in book form and can be quite complex. These rulebooks present two types of information: 1) data about the game world, players' abilities and powers, and typical creatures and monsters, and 2) data about the mechanics that the GM and players will use to make the game happen. Many of these mechanics focus on conflict resolution; questions like "How do I shoot at the bad guys?" "Can I round up the cows with my lasso?" and "Will the pretty lady in the saloon say hello to me?" can be answered through these rules.

Conflict resolution is where dice come into play in most RPGs. Some aspect of the player's character is compared to the difficulty of the task, and this is used to determine the chance of success. The player rolls the dice to see if the activity is successful. After determining if the activity is a success or failure, the GM narrates what happens in the story. There are some RPGs that use other forms of conflict resolution, such as cards, chips, points, or excellent storytelling, but most use dice.

Most tabletop RPGs are cooperative games where players work as a team to overcome challenges. As players work through the story, they are rewarded with money, equipment, and experience. The money is useful for players to purchase things for their characters. The equipment typically will improve the player's ability to deal with the more challenging situations that the GM has in store for the future. The experience allows the players to improve their characters' abilities to allow additional ways of dealing with future situations. These games are not about the GM attempting to kill the characters and "win"; instead, the GM is facilitating a good story-based adventure for the players. Characters may die through poor player decisions or bad luck, but a good GM doesn't frequently kill off characters in most games.

The grand-daddy of RPGs is Dungeons and Dragons. This swords-and-sorcery fantasy game is more than 35 years old and is currently in its fourth major edition. The publisher of Dungeons and Dragons is Wizards of the Coast, which is the same company that produces Magic: The Gathering; it helps libraries run games by supplying games and prizes through its Wizards Play Network (www.wizards.com/default.asp?x=dci/wpn/main). A number of companies, including Wizards of the Coast, produce starting packets with a subset of the rules and a basic adventure.

Over the decades, a number of other RPGs have been developed by both large and small independently owned companies. The ease of web-based distribution allows designers to create an RPG and publish and sell PDFs through distribution sites like RPGNow (www.rpgnow.com). The indie RPG movement has created significant advancements in RPGs in a short period of time and can provide libraries access to inexpensive RPG systems to explore.

There are two main areas of emphasis in an RPG: mechanics and story. Most systems emphasize one over the other, and many players make their choice of a system to use based upon what they enjoy doing. Dungeons and Dragons originally grew out of the hobby of tactical miniature-based battle games, and its system has always emphasized the mechanics of the game. The fourth edition has created quite a stir among the fan base, because it is focused even more on mechanics than other recent editions.

Many of the new independent RPGs focus more heavily on the story element, with simple mechanics that are designed to emphasize the storytelling. For example, 1001 Nights, a game set in the Arabian Nights world, gives players gems, which they spend as they continue the story. Other games that empower players to help create and tell the story are Prime Time Adventures, where players create a television show and cast and then play out an episode of the show, and Spirit of the Century, a romping 1920s' pulp adventure. By giving players more control over their characters and where the story goes, they can become more involved in the experience. Many of these games give players advantages in their chance of succeeding if they tell a good story.

For example, in a mechanics-focused RPG, a player may say, "I swing my sword," roll the die, and report a hit or miss. In a story-focused RPG, the player may be empowered to embellish the situation during the storytelling: "Glancing behind the opponent, I see a shallow mud puddle. I purposefully thrust not to hit him but to drive him toward the slippery edge of the puddle so that I can get an advantage for the future." In these systems, good storytelling rewards the players, as compared to good die-rolling in a mechanics-heavy system. Moreover, a creative GM can create a game more focused on one or the other regardless of the underlying system.

RPGs usually involve much more than combat. Players also work through social situations, solve problems and puzzles, and interact with the game world in the same way that their characters would. Many of these game worlds are set in the worlds of literature very similar to popular literature in the library, such as *Harry Potter*, *Twilight*, and *Lord of the Rings*. One game system, Call of Cthulhu, is set in the literary world of H.P. Lovecraft. The players are investigators exploring powers much more powerful than they, such that combat is deadly and a last resort. This game emphasizes research and social skills and even has players rolling against their "Library Use" skill. A clever GM in a library setting could build in elements where players do actual research using library resources to discover clues to help them in the game.

There are also RPGs for children that have more basic mechanics. One of the newer children's RPGs that adults enjoy as well is the beautifully produced Mouse Guard. Based upon the book of the same name, Mouse Guard has players working together as mice in different roles dealing with threats to their mouse kingdom. Each year, the national Origins game show has a voting procedure for attendees to select the games of the year, and in 2009, Mouse Guard beat out Dungeons and Dragons (fourth edition) to take the award for Roleplaying Game of the Year. Faery's Tale (www.firefly-games.com) is another less complex and inexpensive RPG ($10 for the PDF version), which is easier for children to play.

The biggest challenge to running an RPG is time. Due to an RPG's complexity, both players and GMs have to dedicate a significant amount of time to learn and play these games. The GM has the biggest challenge, as this person must not only understand the books of rules but also must prepare the game world, characters within the world, the story that the players will explore, and the challenges that make up that story. For each session, the GM must plan out new adventures for the players. The importance of this person in running the event means that he or she must be trustworthy, such as a library staff member or a volunteer working closely with the library.

There are some RPGs that reduce the time needed to prepare and play. The Shab-al-Hiri Roach is a game set in a university setting, where players are faculty members attempting to get tenure. The game does not require a GM but instead has players work through a set of six scenes representing the academic year. At the start of each scene, players draw a card that dictates one goal they need to meet during the scene. The entire experience takes a few hours to complete.

Some board and card games also involve players' storytelling skills. In Tales of the Arabian Nights, players use a Book of Tales to lead each other through mystical experiences in a style similar to the old *Choose Your Own Adventure* series. Once Upon a Time has players tell a story through playing cards with concepts on them. As players add a card, they continue the story based upon that concept. A new storytelling card game is Aye, Dark Overlord!, where players are a group of minions who have failed their Dark Overlord. One of the players takes on the role of the Dark Overlord and questions the minions about their failure; they play cards in response to come up with their excuses and pass the buck to other minions. Librarians could easily create this type of a storytelling game with blank cards, where each player creates some cards with their own concepts. The cards are then shuffled and dealt out for the storytelling to begin.

Shab-al-Hiri Roach, tabletop RPG, Bully Pulpit, $20, 2–6 players
Experience: Players take on the roles of faculty members scrambling for tenure with the influence of a powerful evil roach moving from person to person.
Demographic: Teens (older), adults
Complexity: Medium
Minimum Length: 3 hours
Interaction: Social interaction as players play both heroes and villains
Skills: Roleplaying, puzzle-solving, negotiation

Mouse Guard, tabletop RPG, Archaia Studio Press, $29.95, 2+ players
Experience: Individuals play mice working together to defend their homeland against attackers and both natural and unnatural threats.
Demographic: Children, teens (younger), adults (who are creative), seniors
Complexity: Medium
Minimum Length: Up to GM
Interaction: Social interaction, teamwork
Skills: Role-playing, puzzle-solving, teamwork, risk versus reward calculation

Tales of the Arabian Nights, board game, Z-man Games, $59.99, 2–6 players
Experience: One player reads from a Book of Tales and offers another player choices, and based upon the choices, the skills of the players, and some luck, players have a variety of adventures.
Demographic: Teens, adults, seniors
Complexity: Medium
Minimum Length: A full game is 30 minutes per player, but an earlier end can be set.
Interaction: There is little in-game interaction between characters, but players are reading stories to each other.
Skills: Light role-playing, strategy, risk versus reward calculation

Aye, Dark Overlord!, card game, Fantasy Flight Games, $24.95, 4–12 players
Experience: Players are henchmen who have failed their Dark Overlord in a quest and must provide a series of excuses as they relay the tale.
Demographic: Teens, adults (who are creative)
Complexity: Low to medium
Minimum Length: The game is best played to a specific time limit such as 15 minutes.
Interaction: Role-playing, negotiation
Skills: Quick creative thinking, storytelling

Digital Role-Playing Games

As with some digital action and strategy games, many digital RPGs are designed as single-player activities that take many hours to complete. There are a number of formats of these single-player games, from the Diablo-style single-player hack-and-slack games to story-based survival horror games like Resident Evil to the *Star Wars*-themed Knights of the Old Republic to the Japanese-style RPGs like

Final Fantasy to the puzzle-solving RPGs like the Zelda series to the life-simulating Fable series. As with analog RPGs, some of these games focus more on story while others focus on mechanics. While this genre is very popular, the games within it are not appropriate for a multiplayer-focused library gaming program.

There are multiplayer versions of some of these character-development, story-based games, the most popular of which are massively multiplayer online role-playing games (MMORPGs). In these games, players sit at their individual machines and link into a shared world. Players can team up through groups and guilds to work through in-game challenges, or they can face off in player vs. player challenges. The current front-running MMORPG is World of Warcraft (WoW), with more than 10 million players. In fact, there are guilds for Libraries and Librarians on the Aerie Peak server in World of Warcraft!

Our library is having our first World of Warcraft event this month. We have many of the story books, graphic novels, and programming guides that accompany the game in our circulation, so we plan to promote those items during the activity. Our target audience is mostly young adults and college students, although we have received interest from adults in their mid-thirties as well. We think that by getting college students around the area in to see what we have to offer, even beyond the game books, they will become patrons for life.

Loretta Walker,
Marion (IA) Public Library

One program structure for a MMORPG is to have a number of players all log in to the same world at the same time. One library staff member or knowledgeable volunteer then leads the group through the character creation process and some starting adventures. The main challenge of doing this with WoW is that each player needs an account and a software installation consisting of the main program and several optional expansion packs. Individuals can sign up for a trial account, but this requires a credit card; conversely, the library can purchase some shared accounts, but then anyone using these accounts could log in to any other character that has been started with that account.

A WoW program may offer more hurdles than the value it provides, unless it is the ideal match to the library's goals for that program. Other choices reduce some of these hurdles. RuneScape, for instance, is a browser-based game with free accounts. While it is not as popular or as well-designed as WoW, it doesn't require an installation or a monthly fee, and the library gaming experience is similar. Other options include Guild Wars and Dungeons and Dragons Online. Neither of these games charges a monthly fee, so once the software is purchased and installed, players can go online and play.

Another program idea is to sponsor a more traditional presentation or discussion for WoW players. Here, libraries would run the program intending to talk about, rather than play, the game. Given that WoW is set in a massive game world with little formal documentation, players and fans have created impressive suites of databases, tools, and plug-ins that are generated through their contributions as they discover things about the world. There is a stunning array of resources, and to play effectively, players have to learn to navigate a variety of search tools and resources.[1]

A different approach to this type of game is Neverwinter Nights. In this game, a GM can play on one computer, controlling the adventure, while individuals all play at different computers. While this does allow for a similar experience to a tabletop RPG with the computer facilitating rule questions and the flow of play, it removes the ability to be as creative as one can be in an analog game; the digital game imposes more limits. In addition, if the goal of the library is to provide a social experience for players to interact, there will be less interaction if each player is at a separate computer than if all of the players are together.

There are also lighter action-based RPGs, some of which were discussed in the previous chapter. As with many games, these lighter games can fulfill both an action gaming experience and a narrative gaming experience, given the right context. One popular retro-style game in this line is the Gauntlet series, where players slay monsters and build up their characters. This is a good example of a game that includes a story, but awareness of this story is not needed to play. Other examples include the Lord of the Rings console games, Final Fantasy: Crystal Chronicles, Baldur's Gate: Dark Alliance, and Champions of Norrath. While most of these games are set in a swords-and-sorcery world, Marvel Ultimate Alliance allows players to play superheroes and work through missions.

The resulting gaming experience for all of these games will be similar: Up to four people will be glued to one system, interacting with each other for hours at a time, but doing little else outside of their world. These story-driven games are good for helping a small group of players interact but are not good choices for libraries seeking shorter gameplay experience or interaction outside of one game. To use these games as a narrative gaming experience, the librarian needs to facilitate discussion of the story that these games are developing, as it is quite easy to play these games without noticing the story.

RuneScape, web-based MMORPG, Jagex Games Studio, Free, 1 player, and *Guild Wars*, PC MMORPG, NCsoft, $19.95 for base game (no monthly fee), 1 player (*Author's Note*: Both of these are better choices for a library setting than *World of*

Warcraft, but *World of Warcraft* has a much stronger following. Any of these games should be placed within a larger gaming program context.)

Experience: A player travels in a shared world with others, gaining in strength and power to defeat more powerful monsters and complete quests.

Demographic: Children (*Runescape*), teens, adults (*Guild Wars*)

Complexity: Medium to high

Minimum Length: Any length needs to be artificially set.

Interaction: Players can interact in-world with others through chat and working together.

Skills: Planning, resource management, tactical decisions

Marvel Ultimate Alliance 2, console game, Activision, $59.99, 1–4 players

Experience: Players take on the role of superheroes working together to fight crime.

Demographic: Teens, adults

Complexity: Medium to high

Minimum Length: A length needs to be artificially set.

Interaction: Players work as a team in-game to fight and complement each other's weaknesses

Skills: Planning, teamwork, quick thinking

Narrative Strategy Board Games

In addition to the board game RPGs discussed earlier in the chapter, there are strategy board games that can provide a narrative gaming experience. These games have elements that bring people into the story and have them engage with each other within that story through the playing of the game. They are still strategy games and can also be used to fulfill a strategy gaming experience, but the theme is important and interwoven with the gameplay.

To accomplish this immersion, these games typically have more complex rule systems with more exceptions to better simulate a specific setting. While the development of the more pure strategy games grew out of European board game design, the development of narrative strategy games came out of American game design.

The requirements for a narrative gaming experience change as players get older. When children play a game, it is very easy for them to slip into the story behind that world. A game such as Candy Land is a narrative gaming experience for young children; after all, it is *a world made of candy*! For a three-year-old, that is a wonderful world to quickly drop into and think about. As players get older, they require more stimulus to play and imagine themselves in another world, so in these games, the more complex rules and gameplay elements provide players with the structure needed to escape.

There are several different types of narrative strategy board games. One popular type is the adventure board game, which is similar to a light RPG experience in board-game form. The classic example of a game in this category is Talisman, where players in a fantasy world roll and move around, having adventures by drawing cards. Several games have improved on these mechanics over the years. Prophecy allows players to develop their characters more to their liking, Return of the Heroes gives players more control of movement over a large map, Runebound creates different levels of challenges that players can select from as they grow in strength, and World of Warcraft: The Adventure Game applies these concept to the popular WoW game world.

One very popular newer role-playing-style board game is Descent. In Descent, one player plays the Overlord and competes against the other players. This is a tactical combat-based game where players work through a dungeon as the Overlord commands a troop of monsters attempting to stop them. Unlike a traditional RPG where the GM facilitates a good experience for the players, Descent pits the Overlord against the players. The game has a number of scenarios that require little preparation compared to a traditional RPG experience, so it is much easier to run the game once the players understand the rules.

Another type of strategy game that typically has a narrative element is the cooperative game, in which players work together to achieve the goals of the game. While some include little story, there is typically an underlying tale that brings the players together. These games are designed to be challenging, so it is not easy for players to win. In Lord of the Rings, the players are attempting to take the One Ring to Mordor, and in Pandemic, players work together to eliminate four diseases that are spreading around the globe.

In some of these cooperative games, one or more of the players work for the game but in a less powerful way than a GM. In some cases, such as The Fury of Dracula, players know who Dracula is, and the individual playing Dracula is attempting to avoid being caught by the others. In other cases, such as Shadows over Camelot and Battlestar Galactica, players do not know who the bad guys are, and a big part of the game is trying to figure out their identities while still working together to defeat the challenging game. In some ways, these games end up functioning more like a cooperative jigsaw puzzle with a theme, in that the players all have specific roles but are working with a team to manage a set of resources and accomplish a goal.

Prophecy, board game, Z-man Games, $39.95, 2–5 players
Experience: Players move around the board gaining new abilities and strength and fighting enemies with the goal of recovering powerful artifacts.
Demographic: Teens (older), adults
Complexity: Medium

Minimum Length: 2 hours
Interaction: While players may fight each other, most of the time is spent fighting enemies on the board and racing for the artifacts.
Skills: Risk versus reward calculation, tactical decision making

Lord of the Rings, board game, Fantasy Flight Games, $49.95, 1–5 players
Experience: Players work together as the Hobbits to survive a series of adventures and take the One Ring to Mordor to destroy it.
Demographic: Children (with help), teens, adults, seniors, intergenerational
Complexity: Medium to high
Minimum Length: 2 hours
Interaction: Players must work together and communicate throughout the game.
Skills: Planning, teamwork, resource management

Shadows Over Camelot, board game, Days of Wonder, $60, 3–7 players
Experience: One player is secretly the traitor and works against the other players as they attempt to protect Camelot, complete quests, and unmask the traitor.
Demographic: Teens, adults
Complexity: Medium to high
Minimum Length: 90 minutes
Interaction: Players must work together while the traitor bluffs to avoid detection.
Skills: Planning, teamwork, social interaction

Pandemic, board game, Z-Man Games, $34.99, 2–4 players
Experience: Players work together to wipe out a number of viruses spreading rapidly.
Demographic: Teens, adults, seniors
Complexity: Medium

Minimum Length: 45 minutes
Interaction: Players must work together and communicate well to succeed.
Skills: Planning, teamwork

Direct Conflict Games

Direct conflict games provide another type of narrative gaming experience. Most of these are also appropriate for satisfying the strategy gaming experience, but these games have a significant narrative element and players take on different races or characters. These differences have an impact during the game. Such games can make excellent connections to reading experiences when they are based on books. A Game of Thrones, based in the literary world of the same name, has players taking on the role of unscrupulous military leaders, and the mechanisms of the game encourage the same kind of treachery that runs throughout the books. Twilight Imperium, (third edition) is a long galactic battle between different races fighting over military and political power.

Hammer of the Scots is a two-player *block war game*, where players control military forces represented on one side of wooden blocks (Figure 7.1); this creates a situation where a player can see that there are enemy troops at a location, but the identity of those troops are unknown until combat begins. This specific block war game is set in a historical narrative with special rules where certain pieces can change sides to simulate what actually happened with Wallace and the Scots.

Some games in the card-driven game category discussed in Chapter 6 also provide in-depth narrative gaming experiences. The game 1960: The Making of the President, for instance, pits Nixon versus Kennedy in an election. Along with game mechanics, many of the cards include actions based on what actually happened in history along with pictures from the era. The result is a rich gaming experience that immerses players in the situation and issues of the

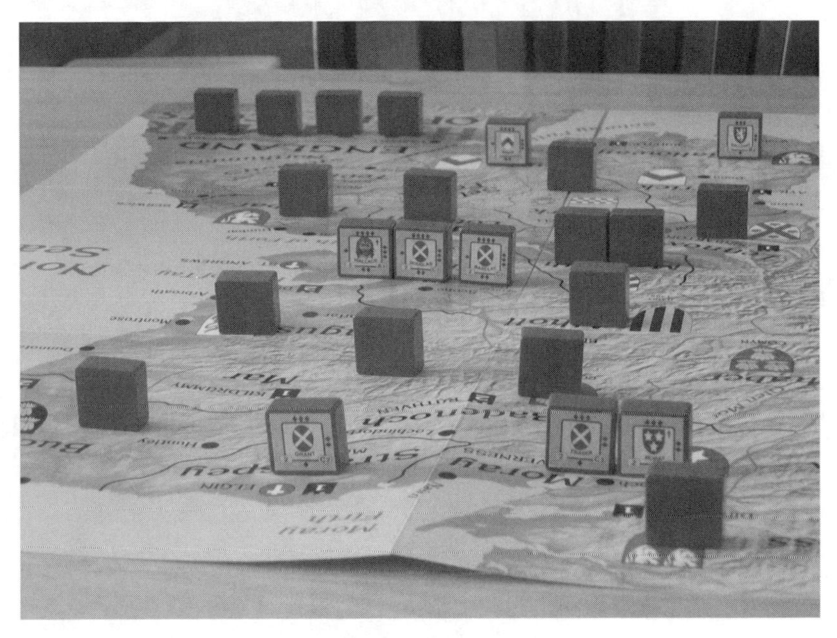

Figure 7.1 Hammer of the Scots (Reprinted with permission of James Fehr)

time. A House Divided provides a similar narrative conflict experience set during the Civil War.

In all of these conflict-based games, the narrative can be emphasized, if that meets the goal of a specific gaming program. The narrative can also be de-emphasized to create more of a pure strategic gaming experience, if that is what is desired to meet the goals of the gaming program.

A Game of Thrones, board game, Fantasy Flight Games, $59.95, 3–5 players
Experience: Players fight over territory with hidden orders to rule the kingdom.
Demographic: Adults
Complexity: Medium to high
Minimum Length: 3 hours

Interaction: Negotiation between players, troop interaction on the board
Skills: Strategic and tactical decision making, negotiation

Hammer of the Scots, war game, Columbia Games, $49.99, 2 players or teams
Experience: Two players or teams recreate the English and the Scots in this historical war game.
Demographic: Teens (older), adults
Complexity: Medium to high
Minimum Length: 2–3 hours
Interaction: Direct conflict
Skills: Strategic planning, historical education

1960: The Making of the President, board game, Z-man Games, $49.99, 2 players or teams
Experience: Two players or teams represent Nixon and Kennedy, balancing resources among traveling the country, working with the media, and focusing on issues of the day.
Demographic: Teens, adults, seniors
Complexity: Medium
Minimum Length: 2–3 hours
Interaction: Direct and indirect conflict
Skills: Strategic planning, historical education, resource management

Big Games

Big games, where the players are the playing pieces in a game set in the real physical world, lend themselves well to narrative gaming experiences. Live action role-playing (LARP) games extend the concept of tabletop RPGs further. Rather than having players say what their characters are going to do, the players actually take on the role of their characters. Players may dress in costumes, take on accents, and create the backstory of their characters within a larger world (Figure 7.2).

In character-based LARP games, players create their own characters within a set of similar guidelines to those for character creation in a tabletop RPG. There is a set game world, and the players create characters that would have a reason to be living in that world. A GM and volunteers develop a story and play the roles of the nonplayer characters, such as the damsel in distress, the forgetful king, and the smelly monsters. Combat may be simulated through real-time mock

Figure 7.2 The author in a LARP game hosted by the International Fantasy Gaming Society

combat with padded swords, or there may be mechanics in the game to simulate combat. Because of the scale of these activities, there are organizations that support them. Libraries can reach out to these organizations and invite them in to run a special event. Most commonly, these games are set within a swords and sorcery fantasy world or in a gothic vampire-laden world, but other worlds such as cyberpunk or H.P. Lovecraft's mythos are also explored. Two of the national organizations that support character-driven fantasy LARP games in the U.S. are the International Fantasy Gaming Society (www.ifgs.org) and NERO (www.nerolarp.com).

Another type of LARP is a story-driven LARP known as interactive literature. In these games, a rich story has been developed and the players play characters in the story. The How to Host a Murder series provide very light versions of these games. In these games, a story has been chopped up into many small pieces, and each player has the backstory of only his or her own character. A player gets a dossier with background on the character, a limited amount of information about some of the other characters, a list of people that the character considers allies and enemies, and goals for the player to accomplish. Through interactions between characters, the story comes to life as players try to figure out what is really going on and how they can accomplish their goals. The GM for these games will control the flow of the game, introducing plot elements and negotiating conflicts.

In my elementary school library, as part of our media literacy lesson, the grade six students played a game about Darfur found at www.food-force.com. After they played the game, they read an article about the same issue (the refugees of Darfur, in the Sudan) and wrote a reflection comparing the two. The students felt like the game gave them a more emotional connection to the story—they cared more, because they felt the fear of running away from the militia.

Diana Maliszewski,
Agnes Macphail Public School (Toronto)

These games have a wide variety of settings, length, and complexity. They tend to be played in one or a few rooms and would work quite well in many library settings where there are multiple small spaces scattered around the library. Many of the games require spaces for small groups of players to meet, exchange information, and conspire. As the game moves along and plotlines get more intense, players can get frantic in attempting to deal with changing situations.

There are a few commercially available games in this interactive literature format that are not in the murder-mystery-party-game genre. Shakespeare in a Box has players take on different characters in *King Lear* or *The Taming of the Shrew* and work through major plot events from the play, which leads to an ending that may or may not be the same as in the original play. Long Live the King has players attempting to win the favor of the king without being tossed in the dungeon for their impertinence.

There are also freely available interactive literature games. The Live-Action Roleplayers Association has a Game Bank online with a variety of games (www.larpaweb.net/gamebank-mainmenu-31). Under the Classic GameBank link, there are two MicroGames designed to be played in 15 minutes as a way to explore this genre of game without a long commitment. This type of game costs little in time or resources and is a great way to explore the genre.

A popular public domain game is Werewolf. In this game, players are given cards at the beginning that tell them if they are an innocent villager or one of the few bloodthirsty werewolves. The game has a night phase where all players close their eyes, and then a moderator has the werewolves open their eyes and decide upon a villager to devour and take out of the game. In the day phase, everyone has to decide upon someone to lynch, hopefully finding one of the werewolves (who are portraying villagers trying to deflect the blame). Day and night alternates until all werewolves are found, and hence the villagers win, or until there are as many villagers left as werewolves, and hence the werewolves win.

Shakespeare in a Box, big game, Workman Publishing Company, $20, 4–10 players
Experience: Players tell the story of *King Lear* or *The Taming of the Shrew* through interaction.
Demographic: Teens (older), adults, seniors
Complexity: Medium
Minimum Length: 1 hour
Interaction: Players work with and against each other to explore the characters and story.
Skills: Storytelling, knowledge of Shakespeare

Werewolf, big game, Public Domain (although published versions exist), 7+ players
Experience: Players take on the role of innocent villagers or werewolves hidden in the village. The werewolves kill off villagers, while the villagers try to figure out who the werewolves are.
Demographic: Teens, adults
Complexity: Medium
Minimum Length: 20 minutes per round
Interaction: Players have to discuss and discover who the werewolves are while the werewolves must bluff.
Skills: Deduction, social interaction

Demographics

Children

Children readily immerse themselves into a narrative world and, with little prompting, will add a narrative layer to any game. With the proper story, even Tic-Tac-Toe can become a narrative battle between the spiky, grumpy Xs and the round, wealthy Os. The challenge with children is complexity; many of these games are complex, and, for children, that complexity gets in the way of the storytelling.

Teens

Many teens do not like to feel embarrassed, and for some of them, the idea of roleplaying in front of their peers is a humiliating experience. For others, the game can provide an escape from a frustrating day-to-day life created by the challenges of a socially driven clique system in high schools. Therefore, teens should not be forced into a narrative gaming experience, but an ongoing narrative gaming experience for a group of teens can be a social support activity for those who don't feel that they fit anywhere else.

Adults

For adults, a narrative gaming experience can be a way to escape back into a childlike state where they can be someone else for a few hours. The complex rule structures in these narrative games allows adults to structure their play; this structure can enable adults to feel more comfortable stepping into a role as they can have a set of rules to guide their exploration. Other adults who are comfortable tapping their inner child can truly enjoy narrative game opportunities.

Seniors

Narrative gaming experiences for seniors are most successful when they have few rules. As adults age, many worry less and less about how others perceive them and just want to enjoy life. Therefore, the same narrative gaming experiences that are successful for children can work well for seniors. In fact, putting these two groups together for a narrative experience can be quite enjoyable and memorable for both groups.

Intergenerational

Some of these narrative gaming experiences do not require the same level of interaction from all participants. For example, in an interactive fiction game, you may have the King and Queen, some nobles, ladies in waiting, a jester, and even the King's cat, all played by different players. A player who wishes to be heavily involved could play one of the major roles like the Queen. A player who wants to be involved but not at the center of the action could play a supporting role or even the cat. This works well with players from different generations and with different levels of interest in the activity.

Library Goals

Narrative gaming experiences support goals involving reading-based literacy and information literacy. They are a natural tie-in to book clubs and other traditional library programming. Many people are hesitant to engage with a RPG at first, so these games aren't the best choice as marketing tools (except to those who are already fans of the genre). Typically, narrative gaming experiences are the most complex of the gaming experiences because the story has to be integrated into the gameplay and embraced by the players. This complexity needs to be taken into account when matching goals to games. But that same complexity creates a richness of experience that can keep a group coming back to the library every week for years to continue telling their stories.

Endnotes

1. Kurt Squire and Constance Steinkuehler, "They Research, Teach, Learn, and Collaborate. So Far, Without Libraries," LibraryJournal.com, www.libraryjournal.com/article/CA516033.html (accessed January 13, 2010).

Social Gaming Experiences

Social gaming experiences focus on the interactions between players. Social gaming differs from the narrative gaming experience in that players in narrative games interact through the roles of the characters they portray in the game. To clarify, in a narrative game, I would interact with you as Wigglesworth, the driver of the Happy Coachman line, while in a social game, I would interact with you as Scott Nicholson. Social gaming experiences allow players to get to know each other instead of getting to know the characters they are playing.

Any game can provide a social experience. Players in a video game tournament can get to know each other during the game or between rounds. During a game of Bridge, players can chat about their lives while they play the game. This type of social discussion can be encouraged or discouraged; some people enjoy having a social experience during a game, and others want to focus on the game itself. The more challenging the gaming experience, the less likely the gaming experience will allow for social interactions.

The class of party games is the common example of games designed to facilitate social experiences. One common factor in party games is that they are not very complex, so that people can enjoy the game and each other without having to worry about the rules. Some of these games have been presented as knowledge gaming experiences; many of the party games discussed in the knowledge gaming experience chapter can also facilitate a strategy gaming experience. For libraries with the goal of raising the level of social engagement among participants, social gaming experiences are most likely to facilitate this.

Environment

Social games are typically loud events, as they focus on players talking, laughing, and getting to know each other. They pair well with snacks and drinks and usually accommodate new players joining the game partway through. First-name name tags for both players and library staff can help create a social space.

We had a simple program of putting out games (already owned by the library) regularly on Saturdays throughout the summer. Teen volunteers as well as staff played with children who needed encouragement or just someone to play with. Children who participated got the reading program theme "tattoos"—play a game, get a tattoo.

Gaming doesn't have to be fancy; you just need to be willing to participate and interact. This makes a nice first or second step for patrons and staff getting to know each other, which makes the library a more welcoming space for the reluctant visitor.

Marf Shopmyer,
Greenwood County (SC) Library

This level and type of noise can negatively impact patrons seeking a quiet library experience, so the place for these games should be chosen appropriately. Noise can have a positive marketing impact, though, as the uproar can entice library patrons who did not know about the game activities but may want to join in upon hearing the laughter and enjoyment.

Party Games

The bulk of games that focus on the social gaming experience between players are lighter games known as party games. Many party games, as discussed in Chapter 4, focus on the knowledge that players bring to the table. Other games focus on some personal element of the players, which facilitates the social gaming experience. For example, in Apples to Apples, one player draws a card with a noun on it. Other players select adjectives from their hands secretly, with the hope that their adjective will be the one chosen by the lead player to describe the noun. Many times, after the lead player makes a choice and points are awarded, the players discuss the various choices available and learn about each other's preferences.

This concept of attempting to match the preferences of a player has been explored in other games. In Gift Trap, players secretly select one of nine gifts for other players and indicate the gifts they would themselves prefer, and players get points for matching others' preferences. In Say Anything, the leader reads a question, such as, "If I could drink only one beverage for the rest of my life, what would it be?" and players write down what they think the leader would say. Each player then predicts which answer the leader will pick, and this leads to the social experience.

There are many other party games in which players have the opportunity to learn about each other's interests. Many of these party games can be played like strategy games, where players amass points without discussing the activity by using the game as a launching point. These games really help with social interaction when discussion is encouraged after each round of play. When library staff members play along, this also allows patrons and staff get to know each other, which in turn can help library staff members recommend library materials of interest. Thus, these games can serve a dual purpose: Not only can they improve social connections, but they can aid library staff in better understanding the preferences of patrons.

Apples to Apples, card game, Mattel, $24.99, 4–10 players
Experience: Players try to conceptually match a lead player's word with their own word cards.
Demographic: Children, teens, adults, seniors, intergenerational
Complexity: Low
Minimum Length: 20 minutes
Interaction: After cards are played, the lead player discusses the choices.
Skills: Reading, predicting behavior

Say Anything, board game, North Star Games, $24.99, 3–8 players
Experience: A lead player reads a question, and other players write answers. Players then try to predict which answer the lead player will select.
Demographic: Children, teens, adults, seniors, intergenerational
Complexity: Low
Minimum Length: 5 minutes per round
Interaction: After the lead player makes a decision, discussion of the answers typically ensues.
Skills: Creativity, predicting behavior

Gift Trap, board game, GiftTRAP Enterprises, $29.95, 3–8 players
Experience: Players select gifts for each other from a set of pictures and then indicate their preferences and score points for matches.
Demographic: Children, teens, adults, seniors, intergenerational
Complexity: Low
Minimum Length: 30 minutes
Interaction: Each player has to think about each other player, so this leads to considerable discussion.
Skills: Predicting behavior

Strategy Games

Some strategy games have significant social elements. One reason for the popularity of The Settlers of Catan is its trading element, where players negotiate with one another. Electronic versions of these games remove the negotiation aspect, which makes the games much more mechanistic. The classic Diplomacy is a game focused on negotiation. In this multiplayer direct-conflict game, players must enlist the help of others to achieve their goals, but eventually one must stab another in the back to win. Another social element in strategy games is bidding. Ra and Medici are different styles of games that hinge on an auction element. Players who do well in these games are those who understand the importance of the social element and manipulate other players into paying more than they intended by bidding higher and higher, then dropping out at the right moment.

Other strategy games feature social elements more prominently. Liar's Dice is a game of bluffing made popular through an appearance in *Pirates of the Caribbean: Dead Man's Chest.* In this game, each player can see only his own die. Players have to make a prediction based on what they think others have, while bluffing about their own holdings. Cockroach Poker simplifies the game to a pure bluffing element—a player passes a card to another while telling him what it is. The recipient can call the player's bluff, or if unsure, can look at it, but then must pass it to another player while stating what it is. Libraries using these games with children or teens should be wary of parents' potential reaction to games based on lying and be sure to put the concept of bluffing within an in-game context.

When matching players to strategy games, it is important to consider these social elements. Some players do not enjoy these types of social aspects to strategy games and want games that are more pure in their strategic focus. Other players find that social elements are what make the game enjoyable; they don't want to play a pure strategy game if it doesn't create opportunities for social interaction. Matching the game to the players is a key part of creating a successful gaming experience.

Diplomacy, board game, Hasbro, $30, 3–7 players
Experience: Players negotiate in secret and write down moves of troops in an attempt to take over other countries. Moves are revealed and done simultaneously, and combat is won by the side with the most forces. Negotiation, alliances, and backstabbing are key.
Demographic: Teens (older), adults, seniors
Complexity: Medium
Minimum Length: 3–4 hours for a complete game, or a time limit can be set
Interaction: Direct conflict and considerable social interaction in small groups
Skills: Negotiation, strategic planning

Liar's Dice/Perudo, dice game, various versions, $15, 2–6 players
Experience: Players all roll dice and keep them hidden under cups. A player predicts how many die of a number are on the table, and other players must raise the value of prediction or challenge the prediction.
Demographic: Teens, adults, seniors
Complexity: Low to medium
Minimum Length: 20 minutes
Interaction: Considerable interaction as players bid, bluff, and call each other's bluffs
Skills: Probability calculation, social interactions, reading people

Digital Games

In most analog games, players face each other, facilitating social interaction. Conversely, in most digital games, players face a screen, and the game rarely requires players to interact socially. As with the aforementioned board games, though, a social context can be added to multiplayer video games through taunting or teamwork. Sometimes this can cause issues: The Xbox Live network is infamous for the level of sometimes racial and aggressive chat that can go on during a game, and libraries need to be aware of this possibility if connecting to others via the Xbox Live system.

Some types of digital games are more likely to bring about a social experience. The first is team-based role-playing games (RPGs), such as the massively multiplayer online role-playing games (MMORPGs) in which players typically communicate with each other through several different chat channels. The World of Warcraft game, like many other MMORPGs, is not a single world but many duplicate worlds that all run on different servers. When players start a character, the first choice they must make is what server they will play on. Players on one server will not typically interact with players on another server. Some servers are labeled as "role-playing" servers, where players are expected to have interactions with other players while playing the role of their character. On nonrole-playing servers, many players will interact with others as themselves—a person who is playing a game—as compared to interacting as their in-game character. Even simple action-based RPGs where players work together, such as the retro game Gauntlet, create opportunities for social engagement.

One game that creates an interesting social experience is LittleBigPlanet for PlayStation 3. Here, players work together to move their characters through multiplatform worlds. Many of the challenges can be most effectively resolved when multiple people work together, but the game is still competitive in that it recognizes the player who achieves the most during a level. The controls are not precise, so that even an expert player still fumbles around a bit, which creates a more level playing field for a new player. The game also has quite a bit of humor, both in the levels and through the stuffed doll characters that players control. In addition, players can work together to create a space for others to explore and, if online, can play in worlds downloaded from the PlayStation network.

One of the reasons for Rock Band's popularity is that participants can play on teams. That teamwork creates great opportunities for social engagement before, during, and after the game. These sorts of musical party games, if played in the right context, can bring about a similar environment to a karaoke activity where people cheer each other on as they play the games. While little in-depth social interaction may take place during the games themselves, due to the noise level, the games create a level of comfort between players that can ease social interactions afterward.

Another social rhythm game to consider is Wii Music. In Wii Music, players use the Wiimote like an instrument. Depending upon the instrument they select, they will wave the Wiimote in a different way. There is no prescribed sequence of buttons to press like in other rhythm games; instead, individuals improvise and "play" as they would like. The underlying melodies and harmonies are played as in the original song, but the music adapts to what the players do with regard to tempo and complexity. There is no scoring mechanism and no way to do poorly; the game is all about a group of people making music together.

I have a hypothesis about digital games and social interaction: The further away players are from the screen, the more likely they are to interact with each other. With Wii games, especially those like Wii Sports that are less intense, players are no longer in "screen space" but are instead in each other's space. This makes social interaction much more likely. Therefore, if the library wishes to encourage social interaction during play, chairs or play areas should be moved back from the screen so that it is easier for players to engage with each other.

LittleBigPlanet, PlayStation 3 game, Sony, $59.99, 1–4 players

Experience: Players explore platforms and solve puzzles to collect orbs and make it to the end. Powerful creation tools also allow players to create new levels and share them online.

Demographic: Children, teens, adults

Complexity: Low for playing; low to medium for creation

Minimum Length: 3–5 minutes for a level, much longer to create a level

Interaction: In some levels, players must cooperate to solve puzzles. Building levels together also requires cooperation.

Skills: Hand–eye coordination, teamwork, puzzle-solving

Wii Music, Wii game, Nintendo, $49.99, 1–4 players
Experience: Players move Wiimotes to control the music played by one instrument in a small combo playing a selected song.
Demographic: Children, teens, adults, seniors, intergenerational
Complexity: Low
Minimum Length: 5 minutes
Interaction: Players musically interact by playing their instruments together and making music.
Skills: Rhythm

Casino Games

Casino games are another type of game that facilitates a social gaming experience. When people talk about *gaming*, they often think of casino gambling—because those in the gambling industry often use the term *gaming* to provide a more family-friendly image of the activity. Many scoff at the idea of gambling in the library, but if legalized, it would be one way to raise funds for the library and bring in a different group of patrons who could then be exposed to a variety of other library resources. Conceptually, this is not that far from using Dance Dance Revolution to bring teens in the library. Real gambling aside, casino games for fake money can be used as a social gaming experience to draw in new groups to the library.

A casino night at the library, where players are given a set of chips upon entering, could be a very successful program for adults and seniors who enjoy playing casino games and would like to do it with little risk. Library staffers could play the roles of dealers and croupiers, making it a point to get to know patrons as the games are played. Poker is a very popular game that is easily played as a social activity. Many popular casino games like Blackjack, Craps, Let It Ride, and Caribbean Stud can be run using purchasable felt mats with payouts and rules printed on them. Small roulette wheels or prize wheels from the Trainers Warehouse can add to the excitement. (The Trainers Warehouse supplies products designed for the needs of educators and trainers and can be found at www.trainers warehouse.com.)

As with any gaming program, a casino night should be used only if it meets the goals of the library, and an assessment is done to ensure that these goals are being met. This type of event might draw attention from the local newspapers and a critical library board, so it's important to ensure the connection between the gaming program and the library goals to avoid bad publicity. Using the event as a fundraiser and awarding prizes at the end may be a great idea or an illegal idea in a given jurisdiction. Be sure that the library follows local laws for games of chance if money or prizes are involved.

Big Games

One type of big game that can be used during a library gaming event to improve the social experience is an icebreaker. These are large-group games designed to let people get to know each other. Some books include hundreds of icebreaker activities, such as *Team Challenges: 170+ Group Activities to Build Cooperation, Communication, and Creativity* by Kris Bordessa or *Team-Building Activities for Every Group* by Alanna Jones. Avoid frustrating players in the middle of the game with an unexpected icebreaker by giving a 15-minute warning before doing the activity. When it is time, suggest to players that they pause their games and encourage everyone to either join in or watch.

Having a formal break in the game action allows the library to have a big group activity and gives it time to make announcements, pointing people to other library resources related to the games that are out for the session. This also can get parents and other spectators involved in an activity, and reluctant players will often join in on the games after the proverbial ice has been broken.

Libraries can also consider doing these types of icebreaker games at the start or finish of other library programs to help attendees get to know each other better. These usually involve physical movement around the space and can serve well to raise the energy in a room before a presentation. Because these activities are also fun, an entire gaming program could be dedicated to a series of these large group games. In this type of program, different types of icebreakers can be selected—some mental and some physical—to keep people more engaged with the overall activity. In addition, if the focus of the gaming program is the icebreaker-style big group games, then more complex games can be used as people get used to working with each other.

Demographics

Children

As with narrative gaming experiences, children can get into social gaming experiences as long as they are not too complex. Children usually don't need an icebreaker to get comfortable in a space and with other people, but these can serve as a gathering activity that takes a group of children involved in many different activities and brings them together around a central activity. More complex social games aren't needed to get children to engage with each other, so the library can design a simple game appropriate for the age group and the topics that the local group is interested in.

Teenagers

Teenagers can turn to social games as a way to get to know other people, as long as the games aren't too silly or embarrassing. If teens feel embarrassed by an activity, they are less likely to fully participate, so librarians should select social gaming experiences that allow teens to maintain their dignity as they play the game. Video games work well with this group, since the attention is more on the screen than on the players. To improve social interaction, a shared evaluation form that the group has to fill out together after playing the game can encourage the group to continue the interactions and discussion beyond the game space.

Adults

A social game structure can work well to encourage adults who didn't previously know each other to talk, as the game provides the topics and reasons to discuss various issues. Casino and party environments are conducive to adults having good social experiences as they recreate social experiences from their typical social settings. Video games may work well as long as they are not overly complex and the adults can just have fun playing the games. Many times, adults are more likely to engage in such activities when there are just other adults there and no teenagers to embarrass themselves in front of.

Seniors

Social gaming experiences can be very rewarding for retired seniors who may not have as many regular interactions with others as they used to. In these games, a player gets the spotlight and gets to share stories or conversations with others; this can be an important experience. Bingo may also draw seniors who typically don't visit the library but who love Bingo; in this way, the marketing goal for seniors is the same as a marketing goal for teens through Rock Band.

Intergenerational

Social gaming experiences can be powerful for intergenerational play. I helped a library set up gaming one summer, and I watched as teens and seniors from the same community got to know each other through these activities. Every event, the same core of different demographic groups would come and talk more and more intensely about their lives and shared concerns about the community. Social games can be powerful change agents in helping different generations learn how others think.

Library Goals

Social gaming experiences are ideal for library goals that involve people getting to know each other. They provide the social lubricant that allows those who share a physical location to get to know each other. Family units can play a game as a group and get to know each other in different way, and pre-existing friends can deepen their friendship through these games. Social games provide the structure that is needed by many to begin a conversation with someone new.

Any game, placed in the right context, has the ability to provide a social gaming experience. Libraries can raise the level of social interaction between participants by using tools such as name tags and rituals such as asking participants at the start of each game to introduce themselves and briefly talk about each game with each other at the end.

PUTTING IT ALL TOGETHER

Now that you have had a glimpse of the breadth of gaming experiences available for the library, it's time to put a program together. Part 3 goes through the process of how to plan, market, facilitate, and assess a library gaming experience. Given the interactive nature of gaming programs and the passion they can incite, there are some opportunities and warnings that aren't typical of library programs. Finally, I present some ways to keep up with the rapidly changing world of games.

nine

Planning the Gaming Experience

Running a gaming program involves more than just grabbing a game and playing. To have a justifiable program that meets library goals, program planning must start with the identification of goals for the gaming program.

Determining Goals

As with all library programs, the mission statement of the library should inspire the goals for a gaming program. Because running a gaming program requires resources that could be used in other ways, a library that cannot develop goals for a program based on its mission should select a different type of program (or change the mission of the library).

Games, just like fiction books, movies, and music, are recreational information resources. What makes games different is that they are participatory; they create an experience that is different each time based upon the players involved with the game. As players interact with the game, the gaming experience changes. Conceptually, this is similar to the book reading experience; a book, the reader, and the reader's mental state will create a different experience each time someone encounters a book. At their core, however, games are containers of information just like other information containers in the library. Therefore, if a public library supports recreational information engagement, supporting games is a natural extension of supporting the changing recreational preferences of a library's population.

Academic and school libraries may or may not support recreational materials through their mission. Many of these libraries do support games as part of their support for the curriculum; some support games in the classroom as a formal connection to the curriculum while others support games outside the classroom as an informal method of imparting a variety of skills through gaming. For these libraries, the connection of games to curriculum is important.

Some academic and school libraries also support the larger mission of the institution in providing social connections between patrons. A coffee shop in an academic library does not necessarily support the mission of the library, but it does support the mission of the academic institution. If the school library is a space for other types of recreational clubs to meet, then a gaming club is a good match for current library users.

Once the match of gaming to the library's mission has been established, the next step is to create the goals for the gaming program. Over the last few years, I have done several surveys of libraries to determine the goals that libraries have for gaming.[1] The next few sections outline some of the most common goals for gaming in libraries.

Attracting Underserved Users

The most common goal for gaming programs in public libraries is to attract underserved users. Once children get too old for storytime, few library programs have been able to keep them coming back. Gaming programs are the next step after storytime and provide a very similar activity: engaging participants in another world through a shared narrative experience. The concept behind this goal is that gaming reaches a subset of the population, most typically those teenagers who don't come to the library because they don't see the library as having value in their lives. A gaming program encourages these underserved users to visit the library and, through appropriate marketing, learn about other library materials. Tied into this goal is repetition; once a library starts running a gaming program, the library should run that program 14 times a year on average. If the library manages to bring someone back in every month, the mindset of that user can change.

There are more types of underserved users in the library than teens, however. According to a 2009 report by the Entertainment Software Association, the average age of video gamers is 35, and 26 percent of people who play games are 50 years and older.[2] Adults without children are another underserved library audience. These adults may not have other social venues, and selecting games appropriate for this audience and marketing to them can bring them back to the library in the same way that video game tournaments bring teens back to the library.

Being a Community Hub

The second most common goal for public libraries is to serve as community hubs. Games are activities that have the ability to cross generational and cultural boundaries. By selecting and marketing appropriate gaming experiences, libraries can create an environment where members of the community can engage with each other in a safe, noncommercial, and nonreligious space. If libraries need to bridge cultural or language gaps with games, then the games selected should not require a specific language or cultural knowledge. Many party games rely upon the knowledge of popular culture, and a library looking to create an intergenerational gaming experience should not use a game that focuses on the popular culture of the last few years.

There are two ways the goal of being a community hub can be implemented. One method is to create activities designed to help a group of people get to know each other better. For example, the library could host a Play With Your Family night, where families come as a group and play games together. Through the games, the library can facilitate deeper connections between family members. Another approach is to connect people who did not previously know each other. Games are great social lubricant, and if placed in a "get to know your community" context, they can work well to help people engage outside of their typical groups. The internet does a great job of allowing people to meet others who share common interests but not a common neighborhood; the library can fill in the gap and provide that place to meet others who are members of the same community.

Providing Entertainment

Another common goal of both public and school library gaming programs is to provide entertainment for their users. This goal places gaming alongside other forms of recreation supported by the information resources within the library. These libraries recognize games as an information resource desired by members of the population they support. Just as users can read magazines, watch movies, or listen to music in libraries, they also can play games in libraries. If the library supports other recreational clubs, then a gaming club fits alongside those offerings.

This goal is served in a different way by a circulating gaming collection, in that a circulating collection of recreational media allows people to be entertained in their homes. It can be challenging to keep a circulating video game collection up-to-date with current available consoles, as the cycle for console development is much shorter than the cycles for other forms of media such as music and movies. The challenge of circulating an analog game collection is tracking the many pieces and cards that some games require to play successfully.

Serving Active Users

The role of gaming in the library is shifting as libraries better understand gaming activities. Over time, gaming is becoming an activity that is integrated into many other library services. Many storytime activities have a gaming component. Summer reading programs commonly have a "Who can read the most books?" game affiliated with them. As librarians become more sophisticated in their understanding of the breadth of gaming, they integrate games more deeply into their library programs, such as using a game as part of a book talk, developing a treasure hunt as part of a special cultural week, or putting selected games on the library's website or computers. While we treat gaming as a special activity now, the day is coming where gaming will be just one more service that libraries offer.

Creating Publicity

In academic libraries, one of the most common goals for gaming is to create publicity for the library. Many academic library gaming programs happen at one of two times during the year: either during the start of the year as an orientation activity or during exam week as a social activity. Students are required to use library resources for their courses, so these programs are more about raising awareness of the social side of the academic library and getting students comfortable with the space, resources, and staff. Some of these programs have an information literacy component, some of them have subgoals of helping the students become comfortable with academic librarians, and others are tournaments that allow students to show off the game skills they have been developing in their dorm rooms.

Many academic libraries are creating social spaces as part of an information commons. This is not a traditional role for the academic library, so libraries find that game programs can draw in patrons, who will then see the other services offered as part of the information commons. Few academic libraries report holding regular recreational gaming programs like those in public libraries. Because of this, their programs tend to be more expensive and elaborate and draw more people on average than public library programs.

Determining the Audience

After the goals for gaming have been developed out of the library's mission, the next step is to decide the audience for the gaming program. The first choice is an audience-specific program for one of the demographic groups discussed: children, teens, adults, or seniors. When creating an audience-specific program, an additional consideration is whether the library will limit attendance to just that group or allow members of other groups to join in. A gaming program marketed to teens may also attract others who wish to play the games.

Another consideration is whether to limit the program to any demographic group or to attempt to draw in members of multiple groups. For this type of program, it will be important to have a wide variety of games so that all visitors can find something to enjoy. A related program is to reach out to groups of people such as families or coworkers and invite them to play games as a group at the library.

Matching Goals and Audience to Archetypes

Once a library has determined its goals and audience, the next step is to select the gaming experience archetypes that will bring about those goals. The audience is important to consider at this stage because different gaming experiences will appeal to different audience demographics. Here are some generalities for the most common library gaming goals:

- Attracting underserved users: Action gaming experiences work well to attract many different types of users. Children and teens are drawn to a wide variety of action gaming experiences, while carefully selected action gaming experiences can draw in adults and seniors. Strategy gaming experiences can draw in adults, and social gaming experiences can work well for both adults and seniors.
- Being a community hub: Social and knowledge gaming experiences work best here, as they both involve interaction between players in ways that more intense games may not allow. An action game tournament where the competition is on display can also bring people together in a similar way to public sporting events.
- Providing entertainment: For this goal, any of the archetypes can work based upon the entertainment preferences of the audience. Action and social gaming experiences are the widest-reaching choices for entertainment, but some types of narrative games that engage large groups of people can work quite well. Just as one type of book doesn't entertain all readers, there is no one type of game that can entertain all players. For this goal, a mix of game archetypes is best.
- Serving active users: The concept behind this goal is that the games are in line with other library services; therefore, the archetype must be related to the service. Narrative gaming experiences can support a book club, knowledge gaming experiences can support a curriculum, and action gaming experiences can work well with a summer reading program.
- Creating publicity: Just as with attracting underserved users, the gaming experience must be matched to the

targeted user groups. Action gaming experiences can work well to draw attention, as they are unusual for a library setting. Narrative gaming experiences, especially the big games, can involve many players at once. A knowledge gaming experience in a game show format can work well to attract attention.

These are starting points, but the underlying concept is that a library has to consider its goal and audience interests to select the best gaming experiences. Also, it is important to note that, in many cases, multiple gaming experiences will be appropriate to appeal to a wider audience. For any group with special interests, the appropriate gaming experience will be the experience that matches those special interests; for example, to attract science fiction/fantasy fans, a narrative experience will work well, while to attract sports fans, an action experience is a good choice.

Selecting Specific Games

After the archetypes have been selected, the next task is to select the specific games for the gaming program. In addition to audience, there are several other variables to consider in making these selections.

Complexity

The complexity of learning and playing a game is important to consider in conjunction with the style of the program and the prior experience of the players. Games have become more complex over the years to keep up with a more sophisticated gaming audience. The Atari 2600 system had one joystick and one button, which has evolved into the Xbox 360 controller with three joysticks/control pads and 11 buttons. One concept behind the Wii system was to return to a simpler control scheme with a Wiimote with motion control, one control pad, and only eight buttons. Adding the optional nunchuck adds a second motion-control device, a second joystick, and another two buttons. All of these controls are useful for allowing games designed for the other systems to be ported to the Wii, but, thankfully, most games designed for the Wii do not use most of those controls.

The same is true for analog games. Over time, some board and card games have become more complex, with 40-page rule books that take an hour to work through on the first read. For many of these games, someone needs to know the rules well enough to run the game, and this can take a volunteer away from helping others with games. Most role-playing games (RPGs) require players to read at least part of a book to play and the game master to read several books, as well as spend the time to prepare each week's adventure.

If the gaming program is targeting experienced players, then complex games are acceptable, and in fact, experienced gamers may already know how to play the games. If the program is targeting players new to these types of games, then simpler games are a better choice. Many simpler games also offer shorter gaming experiences, which match well with a typical public library two-hour open gaming program. Complex games require more time and more dedication, but they can provide a much richer gaming experience if players and the library can dedicate adequate time.

Chance

When selecting games, the role of chance in the game is another important variable to consider. Chance mitigates skill. A game program targeting skilled players should consist of games with fewer elements of chance. If the goal is to create a game program where winning is less important than the play, then games with chance elements are better choices. This is where the Wii infuriates skilled gamers; the imprecision of the Wiimote adds an element of chance to the game and a less-skilled player can win the game more easily. A game like Bingo is mostly a game of chance (and matching numbers to a board successfully) so a practiced Bingo player is not more likely to win than a player new to the game. In a game like Chess, more skilled players will regularly beat less-skilled players.

If a library wants to choose a game with little chance but still wants to create a fairer game, handicapping can be used. Some games, such as Go, have a handicapping system in place to help create an interesting gaming experience for both players. For other games, the handicapping system may have to be created on the fly. A skilled player can enjoy the challenge of fighting against difficult odds to attempt to win in a game. Libraries can take a game that would not be fun for either skilled or unskilled players and make it fun for both.

Competition and Conflict

If part of the core definition of a game is the goal, then part of the game is competition toward that goal. There are a variety of gaming experiences with different levels of direct conflict between players. Some games, such as Chess, Risk, and Super Smash Bros. Brawl, pit players directly against each other; the only way to win is to directly attack the other player. On the other end of the spectrum are games like Dance Dance Revolution and Tetris, where players are individually striving toward a goal and victory is determined by who performed the best. There are many games in the middle, such as real-time strategy games, where players sometimes work in their own worlds and then have moments of conflict with each other. The games selected will affect the tone of the event; for example, games with more direct conflict encourage more aggressive interaction between players. Librarians desiring a less-competitive tone in their events can choose games that avoid direct conflict between players.

Another level of competition in games can be found in cooperative games where players work together to achieve a victory. These games typically have a narrative gaming experience element to them and have either all the players working together, working against one player, or secretly working against the rest of the players.

Space

The available space for gaming is a significant variable in selecting a game. If space is limited with just a few tables and chairs, then card and board games may be a better choice than a Rock Band setup that requires a significant amount of space. Another consideration related to space is noise. If the place for gaming can't be closed off, then noise from the games will travel throughout nearby library space. This might be good, if the goal is to attract attention, or bad, if it interferes with other library services.

Other aspects of space that are important are power and storage. If the space for playing games doesn't have power, then long extension cords will have to be stretched across the library floor to power digital games. (As an aside, gaffers tape is a better solution than duct tape to cover up cords; it doesn't leave a sticky residue.) Another aspect of space planning is game storage; decks of cards are easy to store, while 40-pound metal dance pads for Dance Dance Revolution may be more of a challenge. As the game collection grows, the space needed to store the growing collection of game boxes, spare controllers, and plastic guitars will also grow.

Board game boxes can be problematic to store. If different-sized games are stacked horizontally, then over time, the weight of the games will cause some of the boxes to cave in. Boxes of the same size can be stacked if the corners match up. Another option is to store them vertically. To do this, the lids need to be secured with something less destructive than rubber bands; I use sewing elastic, tied into a loop with a knot. The components inside also need to be contained; snack-size Ziploc bags are an inexpensive way to keep cards and other bits from falling all over the place.

Format

There are a number of possible formats for a library gaming program. One of the most common is an open play event where the library sets up games in the space and allows players to play games with each other over a few hours. From my experience, a 2-hour program works well to bring a critical mass of players together at the same time and not be too taxing on staff and volunteers.

Another option is a tournament, where players are paired off to compete, usually working to win a prize. A tournament will bring certain types of players out, and it's also useful to have some open play activities for players who are not competing and to reach out to those who don't enjoy the tournament structure. Eli Neiburger, from the Ann Arbor District (MI) Library, recommends having a signup available ahead of time to get people excited, although the signups won't be a completely accurate indication of the people who actually show up to the event. However, the fact that people are signing up for the event gets the excitement going and makes patrons more likely to attend.

There are several types of tournaments. The traditional style is a single-elimination or double-elimination tournament, which works best if the library has only one or two stations for tournament games. If the library has many stations for competitors, a round-robin tournament allows players to play many more games during the session. Neiburger hosts a free tool called GTSystem that libraries can use to facilitate a tournament (wiki.gtsystem.org/join).

Another format is to run a long game over several gaming sessions. This is the typical format for RPGs, as the games can run across months or years, in a grand adventure. These games usually have the same game master for consistency's sake, but the players may change from session to session. School libraries can support this type of activity for a classroom, where the class works together over several sessions on a more complex game like Diplomacy or 1960: The Making of the President.

Games that continue across several sessions in a public library can be facilitated through a gaming club. These clubs can be focused on a specific type of game, such as a board game club, or even a specific title, such as a Bridge club. The advantage of a club is that by having a regular session for gaming, players can count on times when they can go to the library for games. In addition, members of the club are likely to be willing to help the library run a large open-play event, as these events are marketing strategies that help grow the club. Getting a loyal core of gaming enthusiasts coming to the library on a regular basis is an important part of the long-term success of integrating gaming in libraries.

Funding

Another consideration in game selection is funding. To avoid taking money from existing programs, many libraries seek funding to start a gaming program from special fundraisers through their Friends group or donations from game companies or local organizations. Libraries sometimes use donated or borrowed equipment from individuals. If a library wishes to use console games, there is a high upfront cost to purchase the consoles, and then a lower ongoing cost to buy the games. Board and card games are much cheaper up front, but if parts are lost, the games may need to be replaced. If a board or card game is still in print, many game publishers will provide replacement pieces for minimal or no cost, especially if they know it is for a library.

For digital games, many libraries already have a projector system that can be used for games, but old televisions can work as well. One challenge with a projector is that the sound isn't usually very good, so the library will need some type of external speaker setup. Any speakers that use a mini-headphone input (as typically used for MP3 player hookup) will work for hooking up to a video game. There is a small connector, typically available at Radio Shack (model number 274–883), that will accept two RCA-style plugs (what consoles use) and convert them to a single headphone-style plug, which goes into the input on the speakers.

Each archetype contains game activities that can be done with very little money. Previously mentioned public domain games like 1000 Blank White Cards and Werewolf would also work. Here are a few additional ideas:

- Knowledge gaming experiences: The public domain game Dictionary can be used instead of the commercial game Balderdash. One player reads a word selected from the dictionary and writes down the definition while other players craft their own definition. The definitions are gathered and read, and players write down their guess as to the real definition. Players score three points if they guess correctly and one point for each person who guesses their fake definition.
- Strategy gaming experiences: Given how inexpensive playing cards and combination Chess/Backgammon sets are, these can be used for a very inexpensive strategy game night or tournament. *Hoyle's Rules of Games* can provide many years' worth of fun with rules to a variety of card games, and a Learn a New Card Game program from this book could teach participants a new card game every week for a year!
- Action gaming experiences: A fun gaming program is a Junkyard Sports program, where household items like balloons and cardboard tubes are used with rule sets inspired by common sports to create indoor games that are inexpensive and fun. Bernie DeKoven's *Junkyard Sports* explores a wide variety of sportlike activities that would provide an action gaming experience. Even something inexpensive like marbles or jacks can work well as part of an action game program.
- Narrative gaming experiences: As mentioned in the narrative gaming experiences chapter, there is little need to purchase a

book with a narrative game world when the library is full of these worlds! A group of people who have read the same book can play a storytelling game where all of the players sit in a circle, and the librarian starts the game by giving the first line to a new story in that world. Each player continues the tale one sentence at a time until the story reaches its conclusion, usually finishing with a round of applause for the creative contributors.

- Social gaming experiences: One commonly used ice-breaker that doesn't cost much is Social Bingo. In this game, the library staff create a five-by-five grid with library-related personal aspects like "Prefers science fiction" or "Doesn't have a library card for this library." Players have to circulate and find people who fit the qualities, and the first person to either make a row (if there aren't many people) or fill their board (with a larger group) wins. Afterward, it is worthwhile to read each of the categories and give the players time to find other people who are similar for future social interaction.

These ideas demonstrate how many different gaming experiences can be created with little funding. One advantage of using the game archetypes model for a gaming program is that the library staff know what type of experience the game is attempting to create. These limits make it easier to use creativity and spare parts to create games that will meet the goals of the gaming program.

Creating Games

Another type of library program with considerable potential is a game creation program. This is currently an underdeveloped area that may grow into a significant portion of library gaming experiences in the future. No matter the archetype, libraries can run a game creation program instead of a game playing program. In a game creation program, the library provides the tools to allow individuals or groups to create games; they then can come back and share their games with other participants, and perhaps, the general public. The game creation program becomes a game playing program as people get to enjoy the games.

We have been running a series of Video Game Design programs that have been very popular and exciting. I believe they do so much toward building media literacy skills, math/computational skills, and storytelling skills.

Christie Chandler-Stahl,
Evanston (IL) Public Library

This can be done in a single session, where teams are given the same collection of odds and ends. They are then asked to create a game in an hour and then share the game with other teams. This could also be an ongoing program, where creators bring their games every week and the group provides feedback. There are some digital programs that work well for this; MIT's Scratch (scratch.mit.edu) is one free tool that can teach basic programming skills as players create a game. Ben 10 Alien Force Game Creator (gamecreator.cartoonnetwork.com) is a free online tool for making simple games based in the Ben 10 world. Several console games have level creator modes, such as LittleBigPlanet and Boom Blox.

There are several other advantages to game creation programs. They teach a much wider variety of skills than simply playing the game, such as creativity, planning, design, teamwork, process-based thinking, and programming. They also can lead to job talks by individuals working in the game industry, introducing possible careers to teen patrons who consider gaming as a primary hobby. These programs can also be much less expensive than buying games but can still provide game playing experiences. If the games are good, these programs can even lead to someone getting a game published!

Endnotes

1. Scott Nicholson, "Go Back to Start: Gathering Baseline Data About Gaming in Libraries," *Library Review* 58, no. 3 (2009): 203–214, librarygamelab.org/backtostart.pdf (accessed January 13, 2010).
2. Entertainment Software Association, "2009 Sales, Demographic, and Usage Data: Essential Facts about the Computer and Video Game Industry," www.theesa.com/facts/pdfs/ESA_EF_2009.pdf (accessed January 13, 2010).

Facilitating the Gaming Experience

As has been emphasized throughout this book, a gaming program involves much more than just games; it is the intersection of games, players, spectators, a library context, and library staff and resources. All these come together to create the gaming experience. It does take work to create and facilitate a gaming experience, but the results create an activity that answers the question: "Why can't people just play games at home?"

Preparing the Games

When players enter a gaming experience, they should be filled with wonder and excitement. Consider a toy store: A magical part of the experience is that some toys have already been set up to play with. Grown-up toy stores, such as electronics superstores, greet customers with row after row of large-screen televisions that allow people to enjoy the high-definition television experience.

The same principle holds for the library gaming experience. Ahead of time, library staff should open up the board games, set them up and sort the pieces, place the rules nearby, and stand up the box to allow for easy identification of the games. Console games should also be set up and turned on, with any codes entered to make the gameplay smoother, and the controllers should be placed on chairs or on a table to indicate to players how to interact with the games.

If the players walk into the space and see board games in boxes and consoles placed next to powerless televisions, they will not feel welcomed. If they are greeted by colorful boards and inviting screens instead, they will be pleasantly surprised with all of the choices, as their prior expectation of "gaming in the library" may have been low. Many will wander from station to station with wide eyes, attempting to figure out what to play but overwhelmed by the choices. First impressions are important, and the first impression of the gaming experience should be that of the potential fun that awaits attendees.

Preparing the Space

Consideration should also be given to the space in which the games are played. Signs throughout the library can point those who were unaware of the program to the opportunity. Games go well with light snacks, but a selection of nonmessy treats is important. Pretzels and M&M'S work well along with water; messy foods like cake frosting, pizza, Cheetos, and wings can be easily transferred from fingers to the games. Another food option is to have messy snacks in a different space complete with a hand-cleaning station. If the program includes action games, exhausted dancers and singers will appreciate having something to drink, and water is a better rehydrating beverage than punch.

Another part of the space should be dedicated to related library resources. There will be times when players become spectators and wander around the space, and that is where appropriate related resources should be close at hand. Books, DVDs, and flyers for upcoming programs that might be of interest can be placed around the food and social areas to encourage browsing.

Finally, a place for surveys and library card applications is useful. As will be discussed further in Chapter 12, it is essential to collect data from attendees for the data-based justification of the gaming program. Also, one typical goal of a gaming program is to draw in underserved individuals, and many of them will not have library cards. The easier it is to sign up for one during the gaming program, the better the chance that participants will decide that it is worth the effort to get a card.

Preparing the Volunteers and Staff

A game program will require staff or volunteers. It is important that volunteers at a gaming station understand how a game is played, how a digital game is started and reset, and how to reset a board game after play for a new group. One way to do this is to bring volunteers in an hour early and teach them the different games as they are set up.

Volunteers and staff play several roles:

- Greeter: When attendees walk in the door, someone should greet them, welcome them to the event, and invite them to enjoy a game.
- Instructor: Players will not know how to play all the games, so a volunteer or staff member will need to be able to teach the game and help players get started. It can be difficult to teach a complex game to new players, but it is a skill that can be developed with practice, especially if someone has the chance to teach the same game to a number of different types of players.

- Adjudicator: Some players will make mistakes or, on rare occasion, cheat in order to win, so someone may need to step in and adjudicate a situation. In a tournament setting, this can be an important issue, and there should be a single head judge who will make decisions. In a nontournament setting, the emphasis should be on fun and getting on with the game as quickly as possible. A coin flip can quickly settle a questionable situation. One common problem involves a missed rule or incorrect rule interpretation, and the choice will be to continue with the game as is or to make a change in a fair way. It is important not to get into a long discussion about rules issues, as this makes the gaming experience less fun for everyone else.
- Security: Wireless controllers, while convenient, are also easy for someone to walk away with. Wiimotes cost about $40, work with any Wii, and can be easily slipped into a pocket. Discs for console games are also small and expensive. If a library has a security system, games and controllers can be tagged to aid with security. One inexpensive security system is to place consoles inside a cardboard box with holes cut for the cables and slots for ventilation. By closing the box, it takes the view of the console away from the players and makes getting to the console to take a disc a much more obvious action. This won't work if there aren't monitors in the space, but as long as someone is there to notice someone opening the box, game theft can be reduced.
- Matchmaker: Volunteers or staff should work to bring people together to play games. They should be aware of people who are not in a game, talk with them about what they would like to play, and connect them with others. They may need to coax players into doing something new or unusual but should also respect a spectator's right to simply watch.
- Player: While it is not the volunteer or staff member's role to play games, some games require a certain number of

players to work well. For example, Blokus is a very popular board game for programs because of its attractiveness and ease of learning, but it plays best with four players. A staff member or volunteer playing in a longer game is taken out of circulation, though, so they should work to bring single spectators into the game to take the open seat.

Facilitating the Experience

As players engage with the games, library staff should work toward facilitating a good experience for as many people as possible. By talking to attendees about games they already enjoy and games they are interested in, staff can make a connection and match players to games and other players. As a board game is finishing, a staff member can chat with the players about what they thought about the game and suggest another game that might be a fulfilling experience.

One pattern that can be hard to break is when a group of people stay together throughout the gaming experience. If one group finishes a game and all other groups are still playing, then the natural pattern is for that same group to start in on a different game. This may or may not be an issue depending upon the goals of the gaming program. If the goal of the program is to help people meet others whom they did not previously know, then staff may need to work to integrate and redivide the players into several groups, while respecting the desires of players who came with friends and want to stay with those friends.

Staff or volunteers may also need to engage in queue management. Popular games may have many players eager to play, and a system for managing them will be important. One method is to create a series of chairs or a marked area for players to stand in line to wait their turn. Another option is to have players sign up and then call their names so that players can do something else while they wait; if a player does not come when called, then that player's name is moved to the end of the list.

To make these programs work, it is important to consider the length of the gaming experience. Wii Golf can be popular, but it can take a very long time to play a nine-hole course, so in a library gaming program, players may need to play only three holes. The board game Wits and Wagers is designed to be played over seven rounds, which can take 45 minutes; a three-round game may be more appropriate for a library program. Testing the games ahead of time will help the library decide how to customize a game to fit within a library experience.

Limiting the Choices

While it might be tempting to pull out every game the library owns, it will be much more effective to only present a few games at a program. If the library owns 30 board games and brings them all out, volunteers and staff will need to understand and be ready to run all 30 games. Instead, a library should select one game and one backup game for each table (in case the first game doesn't work for the attendees). One technique I have used with large groups and board games is to put pairs of identical games next to each other. As one group learns and is playing a game, it can help a second group get started with the same game. When the first group finishes and leaves, a new group can be taught by the second group. This allows the attendees to assist each other, thus relieving some of the running about by staff and volunteers to each table to help with questions.

The same concept holds true for console games. To prepare a game for play in a library gaming experience, certain menu options may need to be selected to put the game in a "No Fail" mode so that players can play through the entire round no matter their skill level. By selecting only a few console games to highlight, games can be appropriately set up and taught. This avoids two potential problems of having a pile of console games out: theft and damage. Loose console discs are easy to take and, at about $50 each, are attractive targets. Someone wanting to try a new game may try to change games without knowing how and can easily scratch a disc, making it unplayable. Extra games should be kept out of sight, and library staff can make the change to a different game if appropriate.

Putting It All Together

Starting with the library mission, the library develops goals for a gaming program. After considering the target audience, the library then selects the gaming archetypes. From the archetypes, games are purchased or developed taking into account audience, space, and funding. A number of games appropriate for the available space are selected for a specific session, and volunteers and staff are trained on those games. Attendees are welcomed and matched to games, and a good experience is facilitated with the goal of the program in mind.

All of this effort is important for a successful gaming program. Once these basics are in place, there are two more elements for the library to consider: marketing the gaming program and assessing the success of the program. While a gaming program can be successfully run without either of these, both are critical for an effective use of library resources to attract a wide array of patrons, to justify these programs as meeting the library mission, and to improve the gaming programs over time.

eleven

Marketing and Partnerships

All the work that goes into creating a great gaming program will be for naught if the library fails to market it. Normal in-house channels and newsletters simply won't reach the target market for a program aimed at those who don't currently come to the library. Because gaming programs are new in many libraries, most people don't think of the library as a place to play games; the marketing of a new service requires more effort than marketing a service that people know already exists.

Just as with game selection, the marketing plan needs to start with the goals of the gaming program. Putting up a generic "Play Games at the Library" flyer, for instance, has a much lower chance of creating a gaming experience that meets specific goals than does creating a flyer targeted toward meeting the goals of the gaming program. If a library's goal is to be a community hub, then its marketing message should convey that (for example, "Come meet others through gaming!"). If the goal is to bring in the underserved, then the message should be something like "Discover the library all over again with gaming!" along with other resources that the library has available for that target group. Marketing messages should be specific to a target audience and a library's goal.

One caveat about marketing games is that many people equate gaming with video gaming. If a library's program involves more than video games, it is important to be specific about the types of games that will be available to play. Along the same lines, when people think of board games, they typically think of Monopoly. This causes many to avoid board games, as their prior experiences with Monopoly may have been unpleasant due to player elimination and time commitment. If the goal is to target gamers, then it's important to be specific about the game titles available.

Reaching Out to Existing Patrons

Marketing a new library service to active library patrons is an easy goal to achieve, as existing channels of communication, such as newsletters and flyers, are already established. Setting up a gaming program to immediately follow another type of heavily attended program can be a powerful way to introduce a new program. After building up a core of interested attendees, the program can be moved to a different time slot to see how effective the technique is in bringing people to the library more often.

Another route to marketing gaming to a group of existing patrons is to fold in gamelike experiences with other services or programs. A small ongoing puzzle hunt in the library stacks might engage the interest of readers who come across the first clue. An icebreaker at the start of a talk can help patrons meet and see how big games work. A Chess board or community jigsaw puzzle can be set up in areas where patrons tend to spend time. In all of these cases, there should be marketing attached, spreading the message, "Enjoying this? Come join us for games!"

Word of mouth can be another powerful marketing tool to help grow a program starting with existing users. This can be done through requests for participants to "Bring a Friend" or can be orchestrated through a team-based gaming experience. Asking for teams of two to attend can help increase attendance, and as the activities will be designed for teams, it can be a chance to help someone with no teammate meet a new friend!

Understanding Gamers

Gaming draws passionate players. Along with fans of comic books, *Star Trek,* and Japanese animation, gamers gather in large groups at game shops and conventions on a regular basis to share their passion for games. Over the last 30 years, I have been one of these gamers and involved in fan groups at a number of levels. Many gaming enthusiasts are willing not only to play their games but also to teach their games to others as a way of growing the hobby. By understanding more about the culture of gamers, librarians can discover gold mines of volunteers willing to bring in their own games and knowledge of the gaming industry to assist the library with gaming programs.

Throughout the rest of this chapter, the term *gamers* is purposefully used with a capital G. Many people enjoy playing games on a regular basis, but they would not consider themselves Gamers. Others, who consider gaming as a significant aspect of their life, have proudly taken on the title of Gamer. These people have probably been gaming in some way all of their lives and game on a regular basis—weekly, if not daily. People currently involved in the activity of playing a game may be referred to as gamers, but those who see gaming as part of their lifestyle will be referred to as Gamers. (For the record, I am a Gamer.)

Gamers at Home

In their home environment, Gamers can immerse themselves fully in their hobby, restricted only by time, space, money, and their housemates' tolerance. For many Gamers, gaming is their primary medium of entertainment, supplemented by reading, television, and movies. Most engage in multiple types of gaming at home, such as playing board games with roommates or family members or playing console-based video games or computer games by themselves or with others online or through massively multiplayer online role-playing games (MMORPGs) such as World of Warcraft.

In addition, most Gamers participate in other information-based activities in support of their hobbies. Gamers read and create many forms of gaming-related media on a daily basis: magazines, books, podcasts, videos, television shows, blogs, and websites. Many Gamers spend more time reading and talking about games through online forums than they do playing the games themselves. There are many forms of information that support gaming, and Gamers learn information literacy skills when working with them.[1]

Many Gamers also enjoy science fiction or fantasy television shows and movies; discussions about an episode of *Star Trek* are not uncommon around a table of Gamers. Some also watch reality television and game shows, as these are televised games. The passion that Gamers have for games extends into other parts of their lives. Libraries can tap into this interest when drawing in Gamers by ensuring that materials on these related topics are available in the gaming space.

Gaming plays a role in Gamers' living spaces as well. Most Gamers have (or wish they had) a dedicated space for games in their homes. This might be as simple as a computer or television area or a few bookshelves of games, or as elaborate as a floor of the house dedicated to games with a room for playing, a game library, a washroom, and a kitchenette. These physical spaces point to an important point of gaming: the social aspect. For libraries to interest the Gamer, they need to offer something beyond what the Gamer has at home.

Regular Gamer Gatherings

Many Gamers gather on a regular basis to play games with other Gamers. Even many folks who play online computer and console games enjoy setting up occasions where they can bring their gaming machines together to play in the same physical space. As gaming is a social activity, many Gamers enjoy the opportunity to play in the same space with each other, taunting their opponents and cheering on their team. Tabletop Gamers require other people to play, so game night is an important social time.

When open gaming sessions are held in a public place, librarians can attend to learn more about a variety of games. Many towns have public gaming clubs that meet regularly, and these are great opportunities for libraries to get to know the local Gamers and their favorite games. To learn about these groups, librarians can check the message boards at local game shops or check online on gaming community websites such as BoardGameGeek (www.boardgamegeek.com), NearbyGamers (www.nearbygamers.com), the AccessDenied.net player database (www.accessdenied.net), and Meetup (www.meetup.com), which lists more than 4,500 different groups under the search term *games*.

Another route to learn about local gaming groups is through building relationships with the management of local tabletop and electronic gaming stores; not only can this be useful in getting donations for collections or events, but it can help in learning the names of different gaming groups and some of the Gamers who lead them. Typically, these groups are open to new players, and Gamers will be happy to teach a variety of new games.

Libraries can engage Gamers by facilitating the social aspect of gaming. When gaming groups are already meeting in public spaces such as bookstores or game shops, they might welcome another venue for getting together. Librarians can invite these groups to host game days or evenings at the library. This provides the game group with a place to meet and helps the library bring in a group of Gamers who are usually ready to help new players engage with the hobby. It also builds a group of knowledgeable advisees who can help the library with game purchases and programs.

Gaming Conventions

A less regular, but still important, form of Gamer gathering is conventions. Most larger cities have some type of gaming convention. These might be tied in with a larger science-fiction/fantasy convention or may be just about gaming and usually run for 3 to 4 days at one hotel over a weekend. These conventions will draw Gamers from a larger area than weekly game sessions. Many of these events, especially the larger ones, will have most of the types of games discussed in this book, so these conventions are great ways for library staff to gorge themselves on a buffet of gaming types over a few concentrated days.

Most conventions also have panels and presentations. One way to reach out to local Gamers is as volunteers to present at one of these events about gaming opportunities at local libraries. Convention organizers might also be willing to let libraries advertise gaming programs. They may also choose to partner with libraries to provide lists of attendees from a specific area for targeted marketing of programs. Most conventions also have a dealers room, where a library could set up a booth to market programs, get volunteers, and talk with Gamers who might be willing to get engaged with the library. If there is no local gaming convention, an entrepreneurial library may be successful in starting a weekend-long convention at the library.

There are two levels of conventions: local and national. Local conventions are usually run by fans, either through individual volunteers or entire clubs, and these can be great opportunities for libraries to find local Gamers. National conventions are very different in that they are typically more corporate and much more impersonal. That said, these national conventions are great ways to learn about many different types of games. Most of these conventions have exhibit halls where game companies demonstrate their newest games. One of the largest volunteer-run national conventions, Origins Game Fair, is held each summer in Columbus, Ohio. It's interested in helping teachers and librarians by providing educators with free admission to the convention, a special lounge, and other related activities.

Marketing to Gamers

An easy way to grow a gaming program is to make sure the local Gamers in your community know about the event—and it would be even better if these gaming enthusiasts were engaged with the planning process. Just as when marketing to any other subgroup, marketing to Gamers requires both an understanding of where they might see that marketing and providing the right message. The obvious locales in which to place marketing materials are game shops as well as comic book shops. Another option is to work with bookstores to put marketing for game programs in their science fiction and fantasy sections. Many schools and college campuses have gaming or science-fiction clubs that can pass along messages. For adults and seniors, gathering places like coffeehouses, churches, bowling alleys, and community centers can be good places to market these programs.

There are many online communities of Gamers. Many allow searching of members by location so these represent opportunities for targeted marketing. There are two routes: Use member search tools to find Gamers in an area or see if there are specific areas to post notices about gaming events. One important note about the latter route is that a library needs to post in the appropriate way for a particular community. Spamming an email list or forum where such postings are not welcome can turn away potential attendees. Just as with existing patrons, the "rolling snowball" strategy is a good one to use with Gamers. Once one Gamer attends a session, he or she can be asked to invite friends to the next session.

Outreach to places not directly related to gaming, like bookstores and coffeehouses, is also important. Many people enjoy playing games but don't consider themselves Gamers and would not visit a specialty game shop. The marketing message for these folks should also be different, focusing more on the general concepts of gaming, games from the past, and a social message about meeting others. Since the marketing message to Gamers should focus on specific games, this means that libraries will need to send two different marketing messages targeted to different groups.

Holding a Regular Gaming Activity

One marketing tool is to set a regular monthly time to hold gaming programs. This allows word of mouth and marketing messages to go much further, as the message becomes "Every Wednesday" or "Every fourth Saturday," instead of a specific date. It also gives people in the library an easy way to market the program when opportunities arise, since it is easier to remember one day of the week than a changing numeric date. This type of regular program makes sense if the goal is to bring in the underserved; regular visits raise the chances that participants will see something else that interests them in the library.

There are several ways to incorporate this type of regular activity. The theme and targeted group could change each month, or the group could remain the same while the library holds several other sessions each month for different demographics. Another method is to have a longer session that is divided in two parts; for example, the program could start with a teen-only session and then move into a session for all ages (which can result in the teens teaching others how to play the games). Another option is to alternate between pure open-play events and a mixed event with a tournament, making sure that players have a chance to learn the game during open play before the tournament.

Developing a Structure

Rather than holding a one-off gaming program, it can be more effective for marketing and prizes to have a larger structure for gaming programs. Eli Neiburger uses the idea of a "season" that runs for a few months, during which players accumulate points throughout a series of activities. These points can come from participation, sponsoring new players, helping with marketing, volunteering, and winning tournaments. At the end of a season, these point totals are then used to earn prizes. One way to award prizes that gives everyone a chance is to turn points into chances to win and then a drawing is used to determine prize winners. If someone's name is drawn twice, that player chooses one prize, and then another name is drawn for the other prize.

Bringing in the Press

Gaming in libraries can be a controversial topic, so the local press may be quite interested in covering the event—if they know about it. As the press may ask, "What do games have to do with books?" libraries must be sure to have gone through the process discussed in this book so that gaming programs are easily justified and tied back to the mission of the library. Another method of involving the press is to use a game-show format involving some local television celebrities, perhaps pitting them against members of the local city administration at a social gaming event that can then be used to market other gaming programs. If a traditional trivia-game format is used, this type of big game can draw a lot of attention without requiring a lot of complex game preparation. Modifying an existing game like Wits and Wagers, however, can create an exciting program where the audience gets to interact with the game as well.

Another option is to create publicity through engagement with online social networks. This could be done by partnering with local bloggers or podcasters to produce a regular column or segment about what is coming up at the library. Another option is for the library to host a podcast or blog and involve patrons as talent. Tapping teens to record a segment for teen programs or a senior to talk about what's going on for seniors can be exciting for both the creators and the listener.

Partnering With Local Game Shops

Local game shops that sell both analog and digital games can be valuable partners; these can also include big box stores that sell games, such as Best Buy. These partners can provide a few resources. First, they can help market gaming activities, especially if the games played are those that they have available for sale to the local community. These stores also may be able to provide contact information for the leaders of local gaming groups. They can provide expertise in selecting games. Once a library has worked through the different variables presented in the models of this book, it will be much easier for the game shop to match games to the library's needs. Just as a good librarian does a reference interview to match a patron to an information need, a good game shop employee does a game interest interview to match a player to a game.

Game shops may also be willing to help libraries administer a gaming program. One common way is through donating a prize—either gaming products or a gift certificate for that store. Another nice giveaway is a percent-off coupon for all participants, which then serves to bring more traffic into the shop. Shops can also help the library by providing volunteers to demonstrate games. Just as libraries offer information literacy courses, many game shops offer demonstration programs that may be supported by the company making the game through training materials and giveaways. The shop also might be willing to bring games to try out for the gaming program, which would be a great way for the library to see which games work well for their patrons before investing.

Partnering With Clubs

Gaming clubs can also be a valuable resource. Most analog games require other people, so clubs are one way that players can find those other people. Members of these clubs can help distribute marketing materials for gaming programs, as well as provide a number of similar resources to a game store: expertise, volunteers, their own games for demonstrations, and networking. As many of these clubs are looking to grow, they may be interested in meeting in the library on a regular basis; if the leaders of the group are dependable, this can provide the library with considerable assistance in offering gaming as a regular program.

Liz Danforth—who has one foot in the gaming industry as a professional freelance illustrator, author, and creator, and another in the library space as a librarian—recommends local science-fiction clubs as another resource for finding people who may be interested in gaming. Many more communities have a science-fiction organization than a gaming organization, but there is heavy overlap between the two groups. Librarians should consider marketing programs to these groups, attending meetings of the groups, or inviting the groups to meet at the library as a way of getting more Gamers involved with library gaming programs.

Other crossover groups include re-enactment groups, such as the Society for Creative Anachronism or military re-enactment groups.

Given that gaming in some forms is akin to re-enactment, Gamers are likely to be found in these other groups. Again, marketing to these groups or inviting them to hold a meeting in the library can help establish a relationship. Along these lines, libraries could market their services and programs at a booth at a community Renaissance Fair or similar festival.

Engaging Volunteers

One of the challenges in running a regular gaming event is staffing, so partnerships formed with volunteers are valuable to the success of an ongoing gaming program. Volunteers can bring in knowledge, games, and enthusiasm for the gaming activity, but libraries need to take care of their volunteers and not burn out their enthusiasm. Working with organizations to find volunteers can also help avoid volunteer burnout, as individuals can trade out with others from the group.

Another way to keep volunteers engaged is to have them help make decisions about the gaming program. Once library staff have used the models from this book to determine the types of games to use, volunteers can work within those constraints to select games they're passionate about. Engagement in the planning of an event provides a level of ownership and pride in that event.

Lastly, ensure that volunteers are able to have fun with the gaming program. Library staff should do the harder tasks and use volunteers to greet, to teach and engage, and to fill in extra slots needed in a game. Volunteers can be asked to set up or to tear down, but they should not be kept too long on either side of the program hours. When volunteers have fun, it increases the chances they will help the library keep regular gaming programs going into the future.

Endnotes

1. Constance Steinkuehler, "Massively Multiplayer Online Gaming as a Constellation of Literacy Practices," *E-Learning* 4, no. 3 (2007): 297–318, dx.doi.org/10.2304/elea.2007.4.3.297 (accessed January 13, 2010).

twelve

Assessment and Justification

The final piece to the gaming program puzzle is assessment. Assuming that the goals for the gaming program are based on the mission of the library, a significant purpose of assessment is to determine how well the gaming program is meeting those goals. Another purpose is to look for areas of improvement to allow the library to meet its program goals more effectively. Because there is a good chance that some members of the public will be critical of gaming programs in libraries, assessing these programs to demonstrate how they meet library goals, and by extension, the library mission, will allow a library to meet those criticisms with data. While games themselves can be fun, the larger context in which the library offers gaming needs to be taken seriously.

Determining What to Measure

When determining what to measure in any program assessment, the first step is to consider the outcomes that the program is trying to achieve. Too many surveys are filled with questions such as, "Are you satisfied with today's program?" These types of "Are you happy?" questions are not very useful in understanding whether the goals of the program were met. People are less inclined to complete long surveys so ensure that each question asked is valuable.

There are three valuable types of evidence to collect from a short survey tool: information about what kind of people attended the program, an assessment of the success of the program in meeting the goals, and suggestions and ideas about future events. A short survey can be paired with some way of measuring attendance through a gate count supplemented by periodic counts of how many people are playing each type of game. If more in-depth data are needed, library staff could be instructed throughout the program to talk with attendees who aren't actively playing about what they like, don't like, and what they would like to see in the future.

Privacy and Demographics

When creating a survey, the first issue to consider is how much personal data to collect. Names and contact information should only be collected if this information is going to be used in some way that is connected to other information on the survey or for follow-up questions. The disadvantage of asking for this on the survey is that it may have an impact on the comfort level of the survey taker in giving honest information. A way to collect contact information while still allowing for an anonymous survey is to have a separate sign-up sheet for people who would like to receive notifications about future library gaming programs.

Some libraries require patrons to have a library card to participate in gaming programs and use a scanning system as patrons walk in to collect information about attendees. If someone doesn't have a card, then they can apply for one when they come to the program. This can, however, have a chilling effect on people who may feel they are being watched, and it may reduce attendance. Libraries should do this only if there is some tangible benefit.

It can be useful, though, to collect some demographic data about attendees. This can be done through observation by greeters as people check in for the program by making tick marks for gender and broad age group (child, teen, adult, or senior). These can also be questions on an exit survey, or both. If data are collected both at the door and on the survey, in the analysis, a comparison will indicate if the survey is more representative of the attendees. It is important to consider how data will be used when developing demographic questions. For example, if there is no added value to asking a specific age, then age is a less sensitive question. Age ranges should be based upon the decisions that can be made; for an all-ages event, age ranges might be broad, but for a children's event, a specific number or very tight set of ranges may be more appropriate. Asking about gender may also be valuable as studies show that different types of games appeal to players of different genders.

Other nontraditional demographics that may be useful to collect involve prior gaming experience. Those who consider themselves gamers may like games that are more complex or require more skill, while nongamers may prefer games with more luck elements. Survey questions asking about someone's prior experience with gaming can be paired with other survey questions to gain a better understanding of attendees to aid in activity selection for future gaming sessions. Asking about favorite games will help libraries see what kinds of games attendees like (and provide ideas for the future).

Another privacy issue involves photographs and video. Given that many games attract attention and may not be typically seen in a library setting, library staff or people from the outside may want to take pictures of the event. A library has to balance this with the right to protect the privacy of patrons who want to play games without having their photos captured. There are several approaches to this.

The first is to have a "No photos or video without prior permission" policy, where anyone taking a picture needs to ask everyone in the picture if it is acceptable. The second is to inform attendees that pictures may be taken of them while attending the event, although this can have a chilling effect in the same way as scanning library cards. The third is to use wristbands: As attendees check in, they are informed that pictures and video will be taken; if they do not wish to be in the photos or video, they need to wear a wristband. While it is the most time-consuming option, it both informs attendees about the photos and video and allows them to opt out. If children or teens are involved, parents may need to sign a permission slip to allow the library to capture pictures.

Assessing the Goals

The next step is to think about the goals of the gaming program and determine what kind of data are needed to assess program goals. The key to creating good questions is to think about the answers that the questions will generate, and then consider the stories that can be told using those answers. If the answers can't be used to tell a compelling story, the questions should be changed. Having goals in mind from the beginning allows librarians to create an assessment tool that will generate usable data.

For example, if a library's goal is to attract the underserved and turn them into regular patrons, then assessments need to focus on providing data that will allow librarians to see how well the program is meeting that goal. To reach that point, the concept of "underserved" needs to be clearly defined (but, hopefully, that was done earlier when determining the target groups for the gaming program). Some of the questions on the assessment tool then need to gather enough data about individuals to know if they are in the underserved category. Some questions could include:

- Do you live nearby? *(This question will allow locals to be considered separately from those out of the area.)*
- Do you have a library card for this library?
- About how long ago did you last visit the library?

If the library runs regular gaming programs, another piece of evidence that is valuable is to track what people do between programs. One way to collect this data on a survey is to include the two following questions:

Have you been to the library's gaming program before today?
- ☐Yes. How many months ago? ________
- ☐Did you come to the library between gaming programs?
- ☐How many times? ________
- ☐No

What did you do in the library between gaming programs?
- ☐Checked out books
- ☐Checked out other things (movies or music or something else)
- ☐Used the computers
- ☐Talked to my friends
- ☐Came for another library event
- ☐Something else

If a library requires library cards for attendees, then it is easy to track changes in behavior. If the main goal is to attract the underserved, then having data about what attendees are doing may be worth the privacy infringement. Another approach is to talk to attendees. A quick show of hands during a break to answer the question "Who is coming to the library more often because of these library programs?" can then lead to a quick focus group interview with volunteers about how the gaming program has changed attendee perspective on the library.

Other questions can work toward discovering changes in attitude. This series of questions can help the library assess if the gaming program is making a difference:

How did you feel about the library *before* today? (Check one.)

- ☐ I didn't like coming to the library.
- ☐ I liked coming to the library, but there was not much for me to do.
- ☐ I liked coming to the library, and there were things for me to do.
- ☐ Or did you feel another way?

After today's gaming program, how do you feel about the library?

- ☐ I feel the same way about the library.
- ☐ I want to come back to the library and see what else is here.
- ☐ I want to come back to the library but only for more games.
- ☐ Or do you feel another way?

Another question to ask attendees is what the library could do to better meet their needs. Again, this could be done on the survey or could be done in a brief focus group meeting. Sometimes, the answers to this question are things that the library already has in place but hasn't marketed well enough. At the next gaming event, requested resources and flyers for requested services can be used as display items around the gaming space.

Questions and tone will be different for a library with the goal of being a community hub. For this goal, the questions should focus more on the social aspect of what people did during gaming. Questions like the following series can help the library understand if the games are allowing people to connect:

> Whom did you play games with today? (Check as many that apply.)
>
> ☐Family members
> ☐Friends
> ☐People I didn't know
>
> If you played with people you didn't know, who were they? (Check as many that apply.)
>
> ☐Children
> ☐Teens
> ☐Adults
> ☐Seniors
> ☐Library staff
>
> Whom did you talk to during the gaming program? (Check as many that apply.)
>
> ☐Family members
> ☐Friends
> ☐People I didn't know
>
> If you talked to people you didn't know, who were they? (Check as many that apply.)
>
> ☐Children
> ☐Teens
> ☐Adults
> ☐Seniors
> ☐Library staff

Therefore, the questions asked to assess the program need to come from the goals of the program. If the library is not able to assess after the first program whether the goals have been met, then the questions need to be rethought. It might also be that a survey is not the best instrument to collect the needed data, so the librarian may have to conduct a focus group or interviews of attendees to gather more data. Or the library may need to change the structure of the program or the games offered if one program is not meeting library goals.

The result of all of this is that the library should be able to answer the question, "Why is the library spending money on games?" by tracing the games back to the goals and mission of the library and demonstrating through data how the games are accomplishing these goals.

Assessing the Event

Another part of the assessment is to understand how well the event worked for attendees. These questions may have nothing to do with the goals of the program but will allow librarians to see if the activities selected matched the patrons who attended. These assessments are not as valuable in justifying the program itself but are very valuable in helping the library adjust a program for the next time it runs.

One temptation in user surveys is to ask, "Were you satisfied?" That question doesn't lead to very useful data, so a more detailed version of that question for an exit survey could be, "List the three games you enjoyed the most today and circle your favorite. If you didn't enjoy any games today, please let us know why." The answer to this request can be used for several pieces of data: the three favorite games, the single favorite game, and reasons why people didn't enjoy games. Some people who came to watch will indicate that on the survey at this point, but some will indicate that the games they wanted to play were always full or there wasn't a game they wanted to play (in which case, the earlier question about their favorite game will help).

Another possible result of assessments is to affect behavior. Consider the following question:

> Did you enjoy the program enough to come again and invite someone else to join you?
> - ☐ Yes, I plan to come again and bring someone else next time.
> - ☐ I plan to come again but do not plan to bring someone with me.
> - ☐ I would come again, but I do not live in the area.
> - ☐ I would not come again to this gaming program.

A question such as this provides a little bit of information, but more importantly, it will affect the behavior of the attendee for future programs by encouraging the person to bring someone else along next time.

A different type of assessment is to count the number of people involved at each game. One way to do this is to divide the length of the program into four quarters, and at the end of each quarter, count how many people are at each of the game areas (including both players and those waiting to play), how many people are gathered around the food, and how many people are milling about elsewhere. When these numbers are tabulated, it provides a total count of attendance at four intervals and provides a good idea of the flow of the event. If the library has chosen to put out a selection of the available games, looking at the flow might help with planning what games go out at what times and when volunteers are needed.

From my own experience from running Library Game Lab events, I find that gaming events are usually slow to get started unless there is some type of activity or event that requires people to be there at the start. Digital games are more heavily used in the first two quarters, and analog games are more heavily used in the last two quarters. Upon entering the space, players are drawn to the flashy video games, and then as they continue to explore, many move to the more social analog games. Attendance is lightest early and late in the session. Knowing this helps me staff my event, decide when to switch some of the stations from digital games to analog games, and indicates that I need the most staff available during the middle portion of the event.

Using Measurements to Evaluate

One goal of assessing a program is being able to evaluate the success of the program. The evaluation process should involve members of different constituencies. Different people will interpret data in different ways and will bring their own value structures to the process. The word *evaluation* comes from the concept of *value*; it is through the evaluation process that measurements from the assessment tools are examined to see if a program is worthwhile.

Library staff, administrators, patrons, and board members should all have a chance to look at the data from assessment tools and discuss which aspects of the program were successful and which aspects need improvement. In addition, engaging these different groups helps more people understand how the mission of the library drives the goals of gaming programs and how those goals are being met. It is also important to ensure that the costs of the program, both in equipment and personnel, are discussed along with these assessments because part of the evaluation lies in determining if the benefit is worth the cost.

Another advantage in engaging these different groups in the evaluation process is that people are more likely to support something that they had a hand in developing. If someone makes a suggestion about a specific game that should be considered, and that game is then used, the chances are much greater that this person will come to see how the game works out or play it along with others.

These groups can also help libraries improve their assessment tools through the questions asked during this evaluation process.

Attentive library staff can learn quite a bit by listening to the constituency groups as they look at data, listening for questions and ideas of what could be asked next time. In addition, questions that provide useless data should be reconsidered, reworked, or removed.

Justifying Gaming

After doing assessments and evaluating the programs in light of their costs, a library may have the evidence needed to justify gaming programs as satisfying its goals and, therefore, its mission. It is also possible that assessments will demonstrate that a gaming program is not meeting the goals, and it is important that this finding be taken seriously. If a gaming program is not meeting stated goals, the program needs to be adjusted. If, after adjustment, assessments still do not demonstrate how a gaming program is meeting goals, the program should be reconsidered.

While games are fun, and patrons who attend games will be enthusiastic, not all gaming is appropriate for all types of libraries. In tight economic times, spending resources on a program that can't be justified as supporting the mission of the library is more likely to draw negative attention to the library. Given that gaming programs can be a lightning rod for criticism, it is essential that libraries be able to justify these programs and educate those who question the value that gaming can play in bringing people to the library, introducing them to other resources, helping them become engaged with each other, helping them learn various life skills, and having fun while doing it.

thirteen

Keeping Up and Focusing on the Fun

Modern gaming changes quickly. Games are a form of mass media, and as such, have the same marketing, release, review, consume-and-put-aside-for-the-next-one cycle as movies. A few games end up having an ongoing life after their first year, but most titles fall out of production so that the next ones can be created and marketed. In fact, many of the titles talked about in this book may be out of print by the time you read it. Digital games that are not self-contained require a computer or console to play, and while they will work as long as a library has a functioning system, the shelf life of these games may be the shortest of any library materials. A 10-year-old digital game collection will be much less useful than a 10-year-old book, movie, or music collection.

This rapid rate of change puts library staff wishing to maintain updated games in a challenging position. Game collections age quickly, and a stream of money is needed to keep games, consoles, and controllers up-to-date if the library wishes to have a game program that will keep the interest of serious gamers. An outdated game collection is more acceptable to gamers who aren't hardcore since their expectations are lower. Only through assessment of their gaming programs can libraries know if the investment to keep up with gaming trends is worthwhile.

Staying on Top of Gaming

The best way to stay on top of gaming is through the web. There are a few print resources available, but they are disappearing as web-based resources take their place. *GAMES* magazine is one print resource that includes a few game reviews each month; its annual holiday review issue (usually available in November) is worth purchasing; it includes its Games 100, which contains 100 reviews of analog games and 100 reviews of digital games. Other magazines to consider are *PC Gamer* for computer gaming, *GamePro* for digital gaming, and *Play*, which has a broader scope and covers the game-related industry.

Some print publications are connected to specific game-related companies. *PlayStation: The Official Magazine*, *Nintendo Power*, and *Official Xbox Magazine* provide up-to-date news on each of the major consoles, but readers must be wary of bias and hyperbole in reviews. *Game Informer* is a magazine published by the GameStop chain of stores, and so it has an expected level of excitement about all products in order to lure players into shops to purchase games.

Some websites have taken on the role of magazines, providing a network of columns, news, reviews, podcasts, and videos. Some of the best for digital gaming are The Escapist (www.escapist magazine.com) and 1up (www.1up.com). The G4 cable television network has a website (www.g4tv.com) with content from and related to its shows.

Most gaming journalism takes place through social media venues such as blogs. Some of these resources are professional, funded through advertising, while others are done by gaming enthusiasts out of love; the line between these two is blurry and not worth drawing a distinction. For digital games, some blogs to consider are Joystiq (www.joystiq.com), Gamasutra (www.gamasutra.com), and Engadget's gaming feed (gaming.engadget.com). For libraries offering programs for children, the What They Play blog (www.what theyplay.com) is designed to help parents understand video games.

For analog games, Boardgame News (www.boardgamenews.com) is an excellent news source about board and card games, RPG Bloggers (www.rpgbloggers.com) is a joint feed of tabletop role-playing game (RPG) blogs, and TCGPlayer.com (www.tcgplayer.com) covers collectible card games. There is a never-ending list of these choices that indicate how passionate people get about games. Following these feeds will help librarians keep up with news about gaming.

There is also a variety of gaming podcasts to listen to and watch. The disadvantage of podcasts over blogs is that it takes more time to listen and watch than it does to scan RSS feeds, but for someone with a commute, these are a good way to stay afloat. Most of the video game podcasts are focused on the typical perception of a gamer and fall into moments of silliness and immaturity. Xbox Live's Major Nelson Radio (www.majornelson.com) is one of the few nonexplicit podcasts and is done by a Microsoft employee that covers a number of aspects of video games. IGN.com (www.ign.com/index/podcasts.html) does a series of podcasts on various video game topics that are also not rated "explicit" on iTunes. The G4 television network does a video game show called X-Play, which has a daily video podcast available through iTunes.

On the analog game side, there are more nonexplicit choices. For board games, the Dice Tower (www.thedicetower.com) has both an audio podcast and a video podcast. I do a monthly review show, Board Games With Scott (www.boardgameswithscott.com), and I am also a voice for On Board Games (www.onboardgames.net), hosted by Donald Dennis, another librarian focused on gaming. The

Spiel (www.thespiel.net) and Garret's Games and Geekiness (www.garrettsgames.com) are two other family-friendly board game podcasts. The Pulp Gamer (www.pulpgamer.com) network covers all forms of analog games through a variety of shows, one of which is called Family Night and focuses on gaming with the whole family. All Games Considered (www.agcpodcast.info) also covers a variety of game types. There is a useful directory of RPG podcasts at RPGPodcasts.com (www.rpgpodcasts.com) and of board game podcasts at BoardGamePodcasts.com (www.boardgamepodcasts.com) to aid in future exploration.

Resources for Gaming in Libraries

A number of print publications addresses gaming in libraries. Jenny Levine edited three issues of *Library Technology Reports* (www.alatechsource.org/ltr/index) that focused on a wide variety of topics related to gaming and libraries, and Beth Gallaway, a consultant who runs gaming programs for teens, shared her wisdom in 2009 with *Game On! Gaming at the Library*. Eli Neiburger's *Gamers ... in the Library?: The Why, What, and How of Videogame Tournaments for All Ages* (2007) is the bible for library video game tournaments. In 2008, Amy Harris and Scott E. Rice edited a collection of chapters on aspects of academic library gaming in *Gaming in Academic Libraries: Collections, Marketing, and Information Literacy*. Lastly, school librarians should read Brian Mayer and Christopher Harris' *Libraries Got Game: Aligned Learning Through Modern Board Games* (2009).

A few specialized online resources for gaming in libraries exist as well. The Gaming in Libraries podcast (www.gaminginlibraries.org), which I host and put together, is a monthly podcast that features regular entries from some of the leading names in the subject. Liz Danforth writes a blog for *Library Journal* on gaming (www.libraryjournal.com/blog/1130000713.html). Terra Libris (www.theescapist.com/library) is a site about RPGs in libraries. For school librarians, one useful resource is SLS Swift6 Games (sls.gvboces.org/gaming), where analog games are mapped to learning standards. Finally, The Librarian's Guide to Gaming (www.librarygamingtoolkit.org), hosted by the American Library Association, sponsored by the Verizon Foundation and Thinkfinity.org, and edited by Beth Gallaway, is a toolkit of gaming resources to help libraries get started with programs.

Finding Reviews

Review resources will also be useful for continuing gaming programs at a library. The profiles in this book are just starting points, but there are full reviews on the web of all of the games discussed in this book. A generalization about gaming reviews is that many are full of excitement and hype about a new game; that game receiving a "10 out of 10" may be joining a long list of other games that also earned a perfect 10. Rating scales are very inflated, so focus on the words and concepts, not the numbers. Most of the preceding resources include reviews as part of their offerings.

The best single review source for digital games is Metacritic's game space (www.metacritic.com/games). Just as with other forms of popular media, Metacritic collects reviews from a number of other resources and combines them into a single score. A similar website focused on games is GameRankings.com (www.gamerankings.com). In addition to the network sites and blogs listed here, IGN.com (www.ign.com) and GameSpot (www.gamespot.com) provide digital game reviews. Giant Bomb (www.giantbomb.com) is a social network-based review source.

For analog games, the granddaddy of board-and-card game review sites is the community-based BoardGameGeek (www.boardgamegeek.com). The creators of BoardGameGeek recently launched RPGGeek (rpg.geekdo.com), which is rapidly filling with reviews. RPGnet (www.rpg.net) is another good review source for RPGs.

No matter what source is used, it is important to collect multiple reviews. One consistent problem with game reviews is that many only consider one demographic: the author's. As has been presented throughout this book, a gaming experience involves a game, the players, and the context in which the game is played. Many reviewers are not thinking of games in this way and focus on only a single context and a small subset of users. A common example of this problem is when adults review games made for children without actually talking to a child during the review process. Because libraries reach out to many types of patrons, collecting a variety of reviews is important.

Keeping the Programs Running

While there will be considerable energy for running the first few game programs, if the program is to become regular, one challenge lies in keeping enough interest and passion going to continue running the events. On one hand, this is a good sign that gaming is becoming a routine part of what the libraries do. On the other hand, it can be difficult to keep enthusiasm going for the program and running it again.

A healthy volunteer base is one way to deal with fatigue. During each gaming program, library staff should watch regular attendees to see who might be a good volunteer. Some people would never think to volunteer and help run a program at a library, but if asked, they may be happy to take it on. Just as with library staff, volunteers can also get burned out running a gaming program. Because of this, it is good to work on creating a group of volunteers, only some of whom are asked to help out during each session. Having different volunteers helps to keep the overall energy level up.

Another way to keep engaged with the program is to change it up. By changing the format, the audience, the games, or how games are presented, the program can stay fresh each time. A tournament will change the tone of the event, as will trying a session with only card games or only party games. Bringing in a game-related speaker for part of the event can be a way to liven things up. There are many free games, and using some of these can be an easy way to do something different.

Adding a design element to the gaming program can drastically change the tone of an event. If participants create games rather than play already existing games, it can bring a new level of energy as both participants and library staff can see the new games created for the program. Adding the creation element adds another layer to the program, which now includes both creation and play.

Doing assessments can help keep a program running. If a program isn't having a clear and measured impact, then those who run the program can grow weary; why should they spend time helping people play when there is a large pile of other tasks waiting for them on their desks? If a program is being assessed in accordance with the goals of the library, the results of the assessment should be shared with those who help put the program together. This allows library staff and volunteers to see the direct impact of what they are doing and can help them to realize the importance of the program.

Considering Legal Issues

Given the growing popularity of a wide range of game types in libraries and the muddled mess of modern copyright and licensing, there are legal issues around gaming and libraries. Games are like other forms of media, so they can be circulated under the same *Right of First Sale* doctrine that the library uses for other legal circulations. If a player installs a game, that player needs to then uninstall the game when the disc is returned for the process to be legal. One difficulty along these lines is that many PC games come with a special installation code and can only be installed on a few computers before the code no longer works. There are some solutions being explored for this problem that are similar to ebook solutions from companies such as OverDrive. Many libraries, if they circulate digital games at all, are choosing to circulate only console games to avoid these problems.

One legal concern for gaming programs in libraries is that of the public use of games designed for the home. There are two issues at play here: copyright regulations and license agreements. Copyright protects the rights of the copyright owner to the exclusive right of public performance of the work. A library must buy a license to show a movie in public, but as of this writing, there is no license available to allow the library to use a game in the same way.

There has been a case where a publisher sued a school for using a board game in a public setting: *Allen vs. Academic Games League of America 89 F.3d 614.*[1] From the ruling on the case: "We conclude that the playing of a game is not a 'performance' within the meaning of the Copyright Act" (paragraph 12)." The ruling goes on to state that even if it could be construed as a performance, there was no charge for the event, and therefore, it would fall under fair use.

Therefore, for many games, this ruling should protect the library when using the game in a setting where there is no charge. There is another issue, however, and that is of licensed music. Many rhythm games use licensed music as their focus, and if the library is playing that music on loudspeakers, it would be easy to extend that to a public performance of the music. Some libraries have chosen to purchase the blanket licenses from ASCAP and BMI (www.ascap.com/licensing and www.bmi.com/licensing) so that they are protected in playing the music publicly. There are many other organizations using these games publicly—churches, schools, and bars—so it is just a matter of time before a lawsuit does occur.

Outside of copyright, there is another issue: the End User License Agreement (EULA), which, in theory, trumps copyright regulations. Many games have these license agreements that specify how they can be used. Many license agreements state that games may not be used for public performances, and projecting Dance Dance Revolution on a wall and playing music loudly through speakers in a public space *is* a public performance. Therefore, it is possible that a library breaking this agreement could be sued. (The legality of these agreements has been questioned in court.)

Libraries here have several choices. The first is to write the publisher and ask permission to use the game in their program. Many libraries have done this and have received permission. Others have received no response but are keeping documentation of this request, which is important for future legal issues. (I have written each of the major companies involved with the rhythm-based games to ask for a more blanket statement about their games in libraries but have received no response.) The second is to purchase the music licenses with the belief that between the prior case about the games in schools and the license to cover the licensed music, the library will be within the law. The third choice is to continue using the games for library programs and deal with legal issues if they arise. The last option is to stick to games that don't have a restrictive EULA.

I would urge libraries to contact game publishers about the use of their games in libraries. This will serve several purposes. First, it will raise publishers' awareness about the number of libraries using their games. Second, it can help protect the library against a potential legal issue. Third, the more requests, the greater the chance that the publisher will act and create some type of license agreement that will allow libraries to use games without legal concerns. The long-term goal is to find the answers to these issues so that games can be used with a clear legal conscience.

Conclusion

Throughout the book, I have presented frameworks and tools to help libraries start with their mission, establish gaming program goals, use those goals to select a gaming program archetype and an audience, select specific games, develop a marketing plan, run a gaming event, assess that gaming event in line with the goals, and justify the choices made for the event through evaluation back to the goals of the program and the mission of the library. I've stressed the importance of partnerships with local game shops, game companies, and gaming and science-fiction groups in getting help both in the planning process and in finding volunteers to help run programs.

There are a few underlying messages I hope you will take away from *Everyone Plays at the Library*:

- Gaming is more than video gaming. The idea that gaming is only video gaming is an assumption that many make, and libraries can help to fight this assumption by connecting video games to other forms of gaming. This makes gaming more approachable.
- Gaming is not new to libraries. In different forms and for different age groups, libraries have been supporting games for more than 150 years. It is a part of what libraries have done in the past and is part of what they will do in the future.
- While gaming is fun, it is important that gaming in libraries meets goals that are derived from the library mission so that the resources spent can be easily justified.
- Gaming can be just one more service that the library provides. By integrating gaming into a variety of other library programs and for different demographic groups, gaming moves from being a special activity to simply one more service that libraries offer. This is an important marketing shift as well, so that patrons will think of libraries when they think of gaming.
- Gaming programs do not have to be expensive. Many gaming programs, especially those focused on game

creation, do not cost much and rely more on creativity than money.

- Gaming is not just for teens. People of all ages enjoy games, and for a growing number of people of all ages, gaming is an important form of recreational media. Children, teens, adults, and seniors can enjoy games with each other in exciting and energizing intergenerational programs that cross traditional demographic and cultural boundaries, or to put it more simply:

Everyone plays at the library!

Endnotes

1. *Allen vs. Academic Games League of America 89 F.3d 614* (9th Cir. 1996), bulk.resource.org/courts.gov/c/F3/89/89.F3d.614.html (accessed September 28, 2009).

About the Author

Dr. Scott Nicholson, MLIS, is an associate professor at the School of Information Studies at Syracuse University, where he runs the Library Game Lab of Syracuse. Before getting his PhD in Information Studies at the University of North Texas, he was a librarian at Texas Christian University. He started the Games and Gaming Members Initiative Group for the American Library Association in 2008, gives workshops around the world about games in libraries, and has written many articles on gaming in libraries, most of which can be found at the Library Game Lab's blog (gamelab.syr.edu/publications).

Dr. Nicholson has also been involved in gaming as his primary hobby since the 1970s and has been active as a board game podcaster and video game reviewer since 2005. He is best known for his internet video show, Board Games With Scott (www.boardgames withscott.com), where he explores a variety of modern board games. He also hosts the Games in Libraries podcast (www.gamesin libraries.org) and is a regular on the On Board Games podcast (www.onboard games.net). He plays the spectrum of games from party board games to World of Warcraft, was a co-author for the Call of Cthulthu Live (first edition) live-scale, role-playing rules, and is the sole designer for the board game Tulipmania 1637.

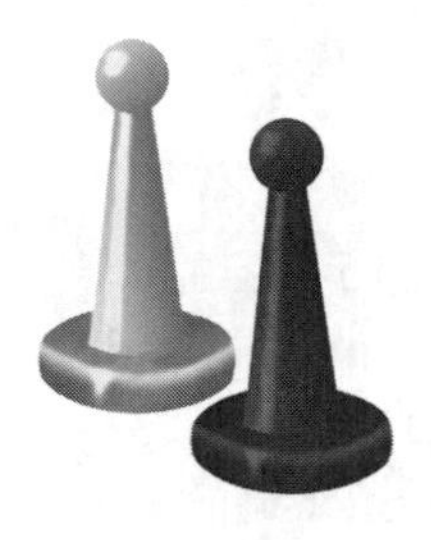

INDEX

A

Academic Games League of America, Allen vs., 208
AccessDenied.net, 179
Acquire (game) profile, 57, 60
action gaming experiences, 81–105
  action elements, 27, 28–29
  analog dexterity games, 98–101
  audiences for, 155, 156
  big games, 102–103
  costs, 162
  demographics, 103–105
  digital, 83–98
  fighting games, 92–93
  library goals, 105
  real-time combat games, 94–95
  retro games, 96–98
  solo-type, 82
  sports games, 89–92
addictions, 9–10
adjudicators, 170
adults
  action gaming for, 103–104, 155
  gaming and education, 6
  knowledge gaming for, 48–49
  narrative gaming for, 129
  social gaming for, 145, 155
  strategy gaming for, 77–78
advertising. *see* marketing
Aerie Peak server, 115
age groups. *see also* adults; children; intergenerational players; seniors; teens
  gaming and, 11

age groups (*cont.*)
gaming experience and, 18
surveying, 191
Age of Booty (game), 74
Age of Empires III (game), 71
All Games Considered, 204
Allen vs. Academic Games League of America, 208
alternate reality games (ARGs), 46–47
The Amazing Race, 45
American Library Association (ALA)
Librarian's Guide to Gaming, 205
Libraries Got Game, 37
midwinter conference, 83–84
Standard Library Organization and Equipment for Secondary Schools of Different Sizes, 37
analog dexterity games, 98–101, 157
Apples to Apples (game), 135, 136
archetypes
development of, 27–30
library goals and, 154–156
area control games, 57
ASCAP licenses, 208
assessments
game maintenance and, 207
of gaming program, 189–199
measures, 189–198, 198–199
sample questions, 193–196
Atari 2600, 96, 156
auction games, 58
audiences
archetype for, 154–156
gaming program goals and, 171–172
identification of, 154
marketing to, 175–176
matchmakers for, 170
for tournaments, 160–161
avatars, game state, 24
awards, 183
Axis and Allies (game), 63
Aye, Dark Overlord! (game), 112–113, 114

B

Backgammon (game), 53, 77, 162
Balderdash (game), 44, 162
Baldur's Gate: Dark Alliance (game), 117
Bananagrams (game), 43, 44
Battleground: Fantasy Warfare (game), 64, 65*f,* 66
Battlestar Galactica (game), 120
Beatles Rock Band (game), 84, 104
Bejeweled (game), 75
Ben 10 Alien Force Game Creator, 164
Big Brain Academy (game), 87

big games
action, 102–103
concept of, 45–48, 176
knowledge gaming, 35
narrative gaming, 124–128, 156
social gaming, 143–144
Bingo (game), 158
Blackjack (game), 142
Blank White Cards (game), 68
blogs, 178, 182, 184, 202–203, 204, 205
Blokus (game), 77, 98
Blood on the Stacks (game), 46
Blur (game), 91
BMI licenses, 208
board games. *see also Specific* games
costs, 161
digital versions, 73–75
mechanics-based, 55–61
scenarios, 16–17
selection of, 16
space-needed, 159
Board Games With Scott, 33, 203
BoardGameGeek, 179, 205
Boardgame News, 203
BoardGamePodcasts.com, 204
Boggle (game), 35, 43–44
Bohnanza (game), 67, 69
books, games and, 5–7
Boom Blox (game), 87, 88, 164
Bordessa, Kris, 143
Brawl (game), 92
Bridge (game), 67, 77, 133
burnout, of volunteers, 206
buttons, 156
Buzz! (game), 41, 42–43
BYTES Project, 40

C

Call of Cthulhu (game), 111
Calling All Cars (game), 91–92
Candy Land (game), 77, 119
Can't Stop (game), 59
Carcassonne (game), 58, 60
card games, 162. *see also Specific* games
collectible, 70
public domain, 67, 68
strategy type, 67–69
Caribbean Stud (game), 142–143
Carnival Games (game), 87, 88
Carrom (game), 99
casino games, 142–143
Castle Crashers (game), 94, 95, 96
Catch Phrase (game), 41
Caylus (game), 58
Chaldler-Stahl, Christie, 164
Champions of Norrath (game), 117
chance, role of, 157–158
characters, game state, 24
Charades (game), 40, 45
Checkers/Draughts (game), 53, 77
Chess clubs, 6, 51–52, 77

Chess (game), 77
  competition/conflict in, 158
  costs, 162
  digital versions, 73
  history of, 53
  marketing of, 176
  U.S. Chess Federation website, 53
children
  action gaming for, 103, 155
  knowledge gaming for, 48
  narrative gaming for, 129
  social gaming for, 144
  strategy gaming for, 76–77
China (game), 57
Chinatown (game), 57
CHITAG event, 78
circulation policies
  displays, 167–168
  for games, 152–153
  for media, 20, 207
Citadels (game), 67, 69
Civilization Revolution (game), 72
Civilization series (games), 71
Classic GameBank link, 127
Classroom Jeopardy (game), 47
Clue (game), 55
collectible card games (CCGs), 70, 77
collections
  games in, 19–20
  rates of change, 201–202
  support for, 19
combat games, real-time, 94–95
communities, online, 181–182
community service mission, 10–11, 175
complexity, game selection, 156–157
computer platforms, 82
conceptual models, 23–30
conflict resolution, in games, 109
conflict simulation games, 61–66
Connect 4 (game), 54
ConsimWorld.com, 65
console platforms
  for action gaming, 82
  costs, 161
  game creation, 164
  security of, 170
control systems, complexity of, 156–157
conventions, of Gamers, 180–181
copyright issues, 208
Cornerstone (game), 98, 100
cost issues, 14
Cranium (game), 40
Cranium Hoopla (game), 40
Craps (game), 142
Cribbage (game), 67
Crokinole (game), 99

D

Dance Dance Revolution (game)
  competition/conflict in, 158

interest in, 83–84, 142
physical skills needed, 81
profile, 84–85
projection of, 209
space-needed, 159
Dancing Eggs (game), 99
Danforth, Liz, 185, 204
databases, multiplayer game, 8–9
decision making, gaming experience with, 17, 27
Deep Fun site, 102
DeKoven, Bernie, 102, 162
Dennis, Donald, 41, 203
Der Schwarze Pirat (game), 77
Descent (game), 119
dexterity elements, 29
Dice Tower, 203
Dictionary (game), 44, 162
Dig Dug (game), 96
digital games
action games, 83–98
costs of, 161–162
focus on fun, 201
rhythm games, 83–85
role-playing games, 114–118
social experiences, 139–142
strategic, 71–76
use of, 197–198
Diplomacy (game), 137, 160
direct conflict games, 122–124
Disaster Game Nights, 40
Discovery (game), 58
displays, preparation of, 167–168
disruptions, in the library, 9
Dodgeball (game), 102
Dominion (game), 67–68
Donkey Kong (game), 96
Donovan, Ryan, 85
Dungeons and Dragons (game), 110
Dungeons and Dragons Online, 116

E

The Ecology of Games (Gee), 16
educational games, 37
80s Arcade, 96
El Grande, 57
Electronic Catch Phrase (game), 42
Empire Builder (game), 59
End User License Agreement (EULA), 208, 209
Engadget gaming feed, 203
entertainment
goal of, 21
provision of, 152–153
Entertainment Software Association, 151
environment
for action gaming, 81–83
home, 178–179
for knowledge gaming, 36
for narrative gaming, 107–108
for social gaming, 134–135
space for gaming, 159
for strategy gaming, 52–53

equipment
gaming experience and, 18
for regular Gamer gatherings, 178–180
Escapist.com, 202
Essen Game Fair, Germany, 78
Euchre (game), 67
Eurogames, 56
evaluations, 198–199
Everything Bad Is Good for You (Johnson), 27
expertise (availability of), 18

F

facilities
gaming experience and, 18
preparation for gaming, 168–169
social areas, 169
space limits, 36, 159
storage space, 159
Family Night, 204
Fantasy Football, 47–48
Fauna (game), 56
feedback, on games, 17
festivals, marketing at, 186
fighting games, 92–93
Final Fantasy: Crystal Chronicles (game), 117
Final Fantasy (game), 115
first-person shooter games, 94–95
Fluxx (game), 67, 68–69
focus, on games, 14–16
fog-of-war aspect, 71
formats, game selection and, 160–161
Foursquare (game), 102
fun, focus of, 201–211
funding, for games, 19, 161–163
Fury of Dracula (game), 120

G

G4 cable television network, 202
Galaga (game), 96
Galaga Legions (game), 96
Gallaway, Beth, 204, 205
Gamasutra, 203
gambling
casino games, 142–143
as game playing, 5
Game Bank online, 127
game creation, 163–165
Game Informer, 202
game market, 13–16
game master (GM), 108–109
game nights, 162. *see also* tournaments
A Game of Thrones (game), 122, 123–124
Game On! Gaming at the Library (Gallaway), 204
game shops, partnerships, 184–185
game shows
audiences for, 156

knowledge gaming, 38–43
as models, 8
staging of, 183–184
game state, representation of, 24
game worlds, games within, 25
gameplay, focus of, 24
GamePro, 202
GameRankings.com, 205
Gamers
characteristics of, 177–181
gaming conventions and, 180–181
in home environments, 178–179
marketing to, 181–182
regular gatherings of, 178–180
Gamers...in the Library?! (Nieburger), 83, 204
games
active users, 153
addiction to, 9–10
archetypes, 27–33
audience for, 154
in collections, 19–20
creation of, 207
definition of, 3–4
focus on, 20
gaming experiences *versus,* 16–18
as information resources, 149–150
instillation of, 207
library audience for, 10
library mission and, 3–12
literacy and, 7–9
maintenance, 206–207
preparation of, 167–168
related library materials, 27
reviews of, 205–206
selection of, 156–163
staying current, 201–205
GAMES magazine, 202
GameSpot, 205
GameStop shops, 15, 202
gaming
aspects of, 18–19
clubs, 161, 179–180, 185–186
conceptual model of, 23–30
conventions, 180–181
facilitation of, 167–173
games *versus,* 16–18
growth of, 6
information literacy and, 7–9
as inspiration, 7
model of, 25*f*
strategy elements, 51–80
Gaming in Academic Libraries (Harris and Rice), 204
Gaming in Libraries podcast, 204
gaming programs, 19–21
assessments, 189–199
focus on fun, 201–211
funding for, 161–163
goals, 171–172, 192–196
justification of, 199
library goals and, 173
limiting choices during, 172–173

gaming programs (*cont.*)
marketing, 175–187
planning for, 23, 149–165
publicity for, 153–154
regular activities, 182–183
repetition, 151
season for, 183
structure for, 183
Garret's Games and Geekiness, 204
Gauntlet (game), 140
Gee, James Paul, 7–8, 16, 27
geocaching, 46
Geocaching.com, 46
Geometry Wars: Retro Evolved 2 (games), 96–97
Georgetown (SC) County Library, 40–41
Giant Pick-Up Sticks (game), 102
Giant Bomb, 205
Gift Trap (game), 135, 137
Gipf (game), 54–55
global positioning systems (GPS), 46
Go (game), 53, 158
Go-Moko (game), 54
goals
of games, 4
gaming experience and, 18
of libraries, 49–50
for strategy gaming, 79
greeters, 169
Guesstures (game), 41
Guild Wars (game), 15, 116
Guitar Hero (game), 15, 84, 85
Gulo Gulo (game), 99, 101, 104

H

Haba games, 76–77, 99, 103
Halo 3 (game), 95
Hammer of the Scots (game), 122, 123*f*, 124
Hamster Rolle (game), 98
Hangman (game), 43, 45
Harris, Amy, 204
Harris, Chris, 37
Harris, Christopher, 204
Hasbro, 55
Hearts (game), 67
Heroscape (game), 63, 64*f*, 66
Hive (game), 54, 55
A House Divided (game), 123
How Computer Games Help Children Learn (Shaffer), 27
How to Host a Murder series, 126
Hoyle's Rules of Games, 162
Huch & Friends, 56
Hula Hippos (game), 99

I

icebreaker activities, 143
IGN.com, 203, 205
Incan Gold (game), 59, 61
information literacy, 8–9
instructors, 169

intergenerational players
  action gaming for, 104
  knowledge gaming for, 49
  narrative gaming for, 130
  social gaming for, 145–146
International Abstract Games Organization (IAGO), 53
International Fantasy Gaming Society, 125, 126
iTunes, 203

J

jacks, 162
Jenga (game), 29, 98
Jeopardy (game), 41, 47
jigsaw puzzles, 4–5, 176
Johnson, Steven, 27
Jones, Alanna, 143
Joust (game), 96
joysticks, 156
Joystiq.com, 203
Junkyard Sports (DeKoven), 162
Junkyard Sports program, 162
justifications, for gaming, 199

K

Kickball (game), 102
Killer Bunnies (game), 67
Knights of the Old Republic (game), 114
knowledge gaming experiences
  audiences for, 155
  big games, 45–48
  costs, 162
  demographics, 48–49
  educational, 37
  elements, 27, 29
  gaming experiences, 35–50
  word games, 43–45

L

Learn a New Card Game program, 162
legal issues, 207–209
Let It Ride (game), 142
Levine, Jenny, 83, 204
Liar's Dice (game), 137, 138
Librarian's Guide to Gaming, 205
libraries
  attracting underserved users, 150–151
  as community hubs, 151–152
  goals of, 49–50
  mission of, 3–12
  resources for gaming, 204–205
  space for gaming, 159, 168–169
Libraries Got Game (Mayer and Harris), 37, 204
Library Game Lab of Syracuse, 10, 197
library goals
  action gaming and, 105
  archetypes, 154–156
  assessment of, 192–196

library goals (*cont.*)
audiences and, 171–172
gaming programs and, 173
justification for gaming, 199
narrative gaming, 130
planning for the gaming experience, 149–154
social gaming and, 146
strategy games and, 79
tournaments and, 79, 105
Library Journal on gaming, 204
Library Mini Golf (game), 102
Library Technology Reports, 204
licenses, 208–209
life skills, 79
literacy, gaming and, 7–8
LittleBigPlanet (game), 141, 164
live action role-playing (LARP) games, 124–127
Live-Action Roleplayers Association, 127
Looney Labs, 56
Lord of the Rings: Conquest (game), 94, 95
Lord of the Rings (game), 121

M

Madden Football (game), 15, 90, 91
Madden franchise, 89–90
Magic: The Gathering (game), 70, 77, 110
Mah Jongg (game), 67, 77
maintenance, of games, 206–207
Major Nelson Radio, 203
Maliszewski, Diana, 89, 127
MAME emulator, 96
Mancala (game), 53
marbles (game), 162
Mario Kart (game), 90–91, 91
Mario Party 8 (game), 89
Mario universe, 90
marketing
to existing patrons, 176–177
flyers, 175
game market, 13–16
to Gamers, 181–182
gaming in, 10–11
gaming programs, 175–187
video game events, 17
word of mouth, 177
Marvel Ultimate Alliance (game), 117, 118
massively multiplayer online role-playing games (MMORPGs), 115–116, 139, 178
matchmakers, 170
Mattel, 55
Mayer, Brian, 37, 56, 204
media, circulation policies, 20, 207
Medici (game), 58, 137
Meetup.com, 179
Memoir '44 (game), 63, 66
Metacritic game space, 205
MicroGames, 127

military re-enactment groups, 185–186
Mille Bornes (game), 67
Milton Bradley, 55
Miniature Golf (game), 102
Modern Art (game), 58
Monopoly (game), 16, 55
Mortal Kombat (game), 93
Motorstorm Pacific Rift (game), 91, 92
Mouse Guard (game), 111–112, 113
Mouse in the House (game), 99
Mouse Rally (game), 99
Ms Pac-Man (game), 96
M.U.L.E. (game), 74
multiplayer online games
  information literacy skills and, 8
  strategy games, 52–53
Munchkin (game), 67
music, licensed, 208
My Word! (game), 44–45

N

Namco Museum Remix for Wii, 96
Namco Museum series, 96
narrative gaming experiences, 107–131
  audiences for, 155–156
  big games, 124–128
  costs, 162–163
  demographics, 129–130
  direct conflict games, 122–124
  environment for, 107–108
  library goals, 130
  narrative elements, 27, 28
  strategy games, 118–124
National Gaming Day @ Your Library, 92–93
NearbyGamers.com, 179
Neiburger, Eli, 7, 83, 92–93, 160, 183, 204
Nerf Wars (game), 102
NERO LARP, 126
Neverwinter Nights (game), 116
newsletters, 176
Nine Men's Morris (game), 53
1960: The Making of the President (game), 122–123, 124, 160
Nintendo Power, 202
Nintendo systems
  GameCube, 96
  Mario universe, 90
  Pokémon collection, 74
"No Fail" mode, 172
noise
  action games and, 81–82
  in the library, 9
  library facilities and, 36

O

Official Xbox Magazine, 202
On Board Games, 203
Once Upon a Time (game), 112

1000 Blank White Cards (game), 162
1001 Nights (game), 110
Origins Game Fair, 181
OverDrive company, 208

P

Pac-Man Championship Edition, 96
Pac-Man (game), 96
Pandemic (game), 120, 121–122
Parcheesi (game), 53
Parker Brothers, 55
partnerships
  with game shops, 184–185
  with gaming clubs, 185–186
  for gaming programs, 175–187
  with the press, 183–184
party games, 38–43, 135–137, 151–152
Password (game), 40, 44
patrons
  marketing to, 176–177
  surveying, 190–192
pawns, game state, 24
PC Gamer, 202
PC games, instillation, 207
Peggle (game), 75, 76
photographs, privacy issues, 191–192
Pick-Up Sticks (game), 98
Pictionary (game), 40
Pit (game), 67
PitchCar (game), 99
PixelJunk Monsters (game), 72
Planet Steam (game), 74
Plants *vs.* Zombies (game), 72
play, concept of, 3–4
Play With Your Family night, 152
players
  definition of, 24
  engagement between, 27
  interactions, 25–26
  knowledge of, 27
  matchmakers for, 170
  roles of, 170–171
PlayStation: The Official Magazine, 202
PlayStation 3 (PS3), 86
PlayStation network, 140
podcasts, 204
Pokémon (game), 70, 74–75
Poker (game), 67
policies
  circulation-related, 20, 152–153, 167–168, 207
  on collection building, 19–20
  game selection and, 9
  gaming experience and, 18
Power Grid (game), 59
press, partnership with, 183–184
Prime Time Adventures (game), 110–111
privacy issues, 191–192
projectors, 82, 161
Prophecy (game), 119, 120–121

public domain games, 162
publicity, 153–154, 155–156. *see also* marketing
Pulp Gamer network, 204
Puzzle Fighter (game), 75
puzzle games, 59, 75–76
puzzle hunts, 45, 176
Puzzle Pirates (game), 75

Q

The Quest (game), 67
Quirkle (game), 58, 60–61

R

Ra (game), 58, 137
racing games, 90
Ravensburger, 55–56
Rayman Raving Rabbids (game), 87
reading, addiction to, 10
real-time games, combat-style, 94–95
recreational materials, 149–150
Resident Evil (game), 114
resource management, in strategy games, 57
resources, for gaming, 204–205
retro games, 96–98
Return of the Heroes (game), 119
rhythm games, 83–85, 208–209
Rice, Scott E., 204
Right of First Sale doctrine, 207
Risk (game), 16, 63, 65–66, 158
risk-taking games, 59
Rock Band (game)
  marketing of, 145
  popularity of, 140
  profile, 85
  social experience through, 28, 29, 84
  space-needed, 159
role-playing games (RPGs)
  action games, 94–95
  analog, 108–114
  blogs, 203
  complexity of, 157
  computer-based, 8
  conflict resolution in, 109
  digital, 114–118
  formats, 160
  goals in, 4
  literacy and, 7
  narrative in, 28
role selection games, 58
Roleplaying Game of the Year, 112
route planning games, 58–59
RPGBloggers.com, 203
RPGGeek, 205
RPGnet, 205
RPGPodcasts.com, 204
RSS feeds, 203
rules, game structure and, 4
Rummy (game), 58, 67
RuneScape (game), 15, 116, 117–118

S

80s Arcade, 96
Saboteur (game), 67, 69
Say Anything (game), 135, 136
schools
  classroom support, 160
  gaming resources, 150
Scrabble (game), 35, 36, 38, 43, 77
Scratch (MIT) game, 164
Second Life (game), 5, 73
security systems, 170, 172–173
Selecta (game), 76–77, 103
selection criteria
  competition, 158–159
  conflict and, 158–159
  formats, 160–161
  for games, 156–163
  role of chance and, 157–158
  space for gaming, 159
Senet, 53
seniors
  action gaming for, 104, 155
  knowledge gaming for, 49
  narrative gaming for, 129–130
  social gaming for, 145, 155
set collection games, 58
settings, of games, 25
The Settlers of Catan (game)
  digital versions, 73
  profile, 59–60
  time needed for, 16, 56
  trading elements, 57, 137
Shab-al-Hiri Roach (game), 112, 113
Shadows over Camelot (game), 120, 121
Shaffer, David Williamson, 27
Shakespeare in a Box (game), 127, 128
Shopmyer, Marf, 134
signs, 168
signups, for events, 160
SimCity (game), 73
simulations, digital, 73
SLS Swift6 Games, 205
snacks, 168
SNAKS concepts, 28
social areas, 169
Social Bingo (game), 163
social elements, 27, 28
social gaming experiences, 133–146
  audiences for, 155
  big games, 143–144
  casino games, 142–143
  costs, 163
  demographics, 144–146
  digital, 139–142
  environment of, 134–135
  for Gamers, 178–180
  games and, 16
  interactions, 25–27
  library goals, 146
  party games, 135–137
  strategy games, 137–139
social media, 202–203
Society for Creative Anachronism, 185
Sorry Sliders (game), 99, 100–101

space
  library facilities and, 36
  preparation for gaming, 167–169
Spades (game), 67
spectators
  definition of, 24
  interactions between, 26
The Spiel, 204
Spirit of the Century (game), 111
SpongeBob SquarePants Fact or Fishy DVD game, 48
sports, as games, 5
sports games, 89–92
staff
  engagement of, 26–27
  involvement of, 24
  preparation for gaming, 169–171
  recruiting role of, 206
  reviewing evaluations, 198
  views on the gaming experience, 21
  working with volunteers, 186
Standard Library Organization and Equipment for Secondary Schools of Different Sizes (ALA), 37
StarCraft (game), 71, 72
stock market games, 57
Stone Age (game), 58
storage, space-needed, 159
stories, in game worlds, 25
storytime
  gaming experience and, 17–18
  story selection and, 18
strategy gaming experiences, 51–80
  abstract games, 53–55
  card games, 67–69, 70
  costs, 162
  demographics, 76–78
  digital, militaristic, 71–72
  digital board games, 73–75
  digital simulations, 73
  elements, 27, 29–30
  library goals, 79
  mechanics-based board games, 55–61
  narrative, 118–124
  puzzle games, 75–76
  social, 137–139
  war games, 61–66
Street Fighter II (game), 93
structure, games and, 4
Suitcase Detectives (game), 56
summer reading games, 6, 153
Super Smash Bros. Brawl (game), 92, 93, 158
Super Street Fighter II HD Turbo Remix (game), 93
survey tools, 190
  demographics and, 190–192
  privacy issues, 190–192
  sample questions, 193–196
Survivor, 45
symbols, manipulation of, 7

T

Take It Easy (game), 59
Tales of the Arabian Nights (game), 112, 114
TCGPlayer.com, 203
Team-Building Activities for Every Group (Jones), 143
Team Challenges (Bordessa), 143
team environments. *see also* social gaming experiences
  intergenerational, 49
  for knowledge gaming, 36
  for strategy gaming, 52–53, 56
Teen Second Life, 73
teens
  action gaming for, 103, 155
  knowledge gaming for, 48
  narrative gaming for, 129
  simulation games for, 73
  social gaming for, 144–145
  strategy gaming for, 77
television, reality shows, 45
Terra Libris, 204
Tetris (game), 158
Tetris Party (game), 75
Thinkfinity.org, 205
Tic-Tac-Toe (game), 129
Tichu (game), 67
Ticket to Ride (game)
  adult audiences for, 77–78
  assistance with rules of, 16
  digital versions, 73
  profile, 60
  scoring, 58
  set collection mechanic in, 59
Tier auf Tier (game), 77, 99, 101
tile placement games, 58
time blocks
  game complexity and, 157
  for games, 16
  gaming experience and, 18
TimeSplitters 2 (game), 94
tournaments
  action games, 82, 83, 155
  adjudicators, 170
  audiences for, 160–161
  Chess, 52, 77
  costs, 162
  game selection, 82
  The Gathering, 77
  library goals and, 79, 105
  Madden Football and, 90
  Mario Kart, 91
  online *versus* library, 93
  Peggle, 76, 78
  Pokémon, 74
  prizes, 70, 160, 183
  puzzle games, 75
  resources, 204
  Scrabble, 43
  social interactions and, 53–54
  teens and, 77, 103
  types of, 160–161
  video games, 83, 133, 151
  Wii games, 86

tower defense, 71–72, 72
trading games, 57. *see also* *Specific* games
Trainers Warehouse, 47, 143
trivia games, 38–43
Trivial Pursuit (game), 35, 39, 41
Triviathon (game), 40*f*, 42
Tulipomania (game), 57
Tumblin' Dice 1637 (game), 99, 101, 104
Twilight Imperium (game), 122

U

Ubongo (game), 59, 61
University of Dubuque (IA), 47–48
Uno (games), 67
1up.com, 202
U.S. Chess Federation, 53

V

Verizon Foundation, 205
video games
  action gaming experience and, 28–29
  advertising events for, 17
  circulation of, 152–153
  hookups, 161
  tournaments, 151
  violence in, 9, 19
videos, privacy issues, 191–192
Villa Paletti (game), 98, 100
violence, in video games, 9, 19
volunteers
  burnout, 206
  engagement of, 186
  Gamers as, 180
  gaming experience and, 18
  interactions with, 26
  preparation for gaming, 169–171
  recruiting of, 206
  reviewing evaluations, 198

W

Waelchli, Paul, 48
Walker, Loretta, 115
war games, 61–66, 71
Warcraft III (game), 71, 72
Warhammer 40K (game), 64
WarioWare franchise, 87
Water Warfare (game), 94
Werewolf (game), 127, 128, 162
What They Play blog, 203
What Video Games Have to Teach Us About Learning and Literacy (Gee), 7–8, 27
Wheel of Fortune (game), 41, 43
Wii Bowling (game), 104
Wii games, 85–89
Wii Motion Plus, 86
Wii Music (game), 89, 140, 142
Wii Sports (game), 83, 85, 87–88, 141

Wii systems
controls, 156–157
costs, 170
security of, 170
Wiimotes, 86, 140–141, 157–158, 170
Wits and Wagers (game), 40, 41–42, 172, 184
Wizards of the Coast, 110
Wizards Play Network, 70, 110
word games, 43–45
word of mouth marketing, 177
Word on the Street (game), 44, 45
worker placement games, 58
World of Warcraft: The Adventure Game (game), 119
World of Warcraft (game), 15, 70, 115, 139
Worms series (games), 75, 76

X

X-Play show, 203
Xbox 360, 86, 156
Xbox Live, 73, 139, 203

Y

You Don't Know Jack (game), 41
YuGiHo! (game), 70

More Great Books from Information Today, Inc.

Blogging and RSS, 2nd Edition

A Librarian's Guide

By Michael P. Sauers

In this fully updated second edition of his popular book, Michael P. Sauers shows how blogging and RSS technology can be easily and successfully used by libraries and librarians. In addition to providing easy-to-follow instructions for creating, publishing, and syndicating a blog using free web-based services, software, RSS feeds, and aggregators, Sauers covers new tools and services, introduces library blogs and bloggers, and includes a new chapter on microblogging with Twitter.

304 pp/softbound/ISBN 978-1-57387-399-4 $35.00

Information Nation

Education and Careers in the Emerging Information Professions

By Jeffrey M. Stanton, Indira R. Guzman, and Kathryn R. Stam

Information and IT are central to virtually every industry in which the U.S. plays a leadership role. Here, three dedicated educators present research on students and workers in the information professions. They look at barriers to inclusion and retention, analyze the forces that prevent high school and college students from gaining needed interdisciplinary skills, and tell the stories of a diverse group of students who are thriving in new majors and new jobs.

224 pp/softbound/ISBN 978-1-57387-401-9 $35.00